Mental Health ~~Law Online~~

Annual Revi

GW00392904

Introduction

Mental Health Law Online is the internet resource on mental health law, and mental capacity law, for England & Wales. The home page is at www.mentalhealthlaw.co.uk

The Annual Review 2020 contains all news items, arranged thematically, which were added to the website during 2020.

Chapters 1, 2 and 3 reflect the structure of the website by covering cases, legislation and resources. Chapter 4 contains an article originally published in *Legal Action* magazine which summarises some important mental health law cases from 2020.

Each item beside a bullet point is associated with a website page, which can be located by using the website search function.

About Mental Health Law Online

Features of Mental Health Law Online include:

- **CPD scheme.** Obtain 12 CPD points per year by completing online multiple-choice questionnaires based on monthly updates.

    - The scheme is primarily aimed at mental health solicitors, and is an ideal way to evidence your continued competence, but is also suitable for barristers, psychiatrists, social workers and psychiatric nurses.

    - The course will cover LAA category supervisors, and members of the Law Society's mental health and mental capacity accreditation schemes, for their mandatory CPD hours.

- **Email updates.** You can choose to receive emails on a monthly or more frequent basis.

- **Email discussion list.** Discuss all aspects of mental health and capacity law. This list can be joined by mental health practitioners.

- **Online forum.** The new forum, launched in October 2020, can be joined by anyone interested in mental health and capacity law.

- **Magic Book.** This is a database of contact details, with everything from experts to hospitals and courts, to which anyone can contribute.

- **Event and job advertisements.** Events and job vacancies can be listed for a small fee (no fee for free events).

- **Books.** A selection of books is available from the online bookshop.

- **New, faster website server.** Pages now load in a fraction of a second, following November 2020's move to a new server.

Acknowledgements

Thanks are owed to the following for providing judgments which previously had remained unpublished.

- Ben Conroy (Conroys Solicitors): *AD'A v Cornwall Partnership NHS Foundation Trust* [2020] UKUT 110 (AAC), *Re B* [2020] MHLO 18 (FTT) and *Re C* [2020] MHLO 48 (FTT).

- Liz Conroy (Conroys Solicitors): *Re D* [2020] MHLO 51 (FTT).

- Richard Jones (Blake Morgan): *MC v Cygnet Behavioural Health Ltd* [2020] UKUT 230 (AAC).

- John Lancaster (GHP Legal): *PM v Midlands Partnership NHS Foundation Trust* [2020] UKUT 69 (AAC) (plus a detailed summary).

- Kate Luscombe (Abbotstone Law): *AR v West London NHS Trust* [2020] UKUT 273 (AAC).

- Roger Pezzani (Garden Court Chambers): *AD'A v Cornwall Partnership NHS Foundation Trust* [2020] UKUT 110 (AAC).

- Karen Wolton (Wolton & Co Solicitors): *GL v Elysium Healthcare* [2020] UKUT 308 (AAC) and *Re E* [2020] MHLO 52 (FTT).

Copyright and disclaimer

(c) Jonathan Wilson. See www.mentalhealthlaw.co.uk/Copyrights

Every effort has been made to ensure accuracy, but no legal liability for errors or omissions is accepted. If you require legal advice then please speak with a lawyer rather than rely on this document.

Contents

1 Cases

All 2020 cases (including any added since this booklet was published) can be browsed on the database at: www.mhlo.uk/cg.

Where text appears within quotation marks, it is a direct quotation from the judgment rather than a summary.

Case pages on the website usually have a link to the written judgment, and often to more detailed summaries and law reports such as the Weekly Law Reports (Daily).

The abbreviations used in case citations include:

- FTT – First-tier Tribunal

- UKUT – Upper Tribunal

  - AAC – Administrative Appeals Chamber

- EWCOP or COP – Court of Protection

- EWHC – High Court

  - Admin – Administrative Court

  - Ch – Chancery Division

  - QBD – Queen's Bench Division

- EWCA – Court of Appeal

- UKSC – Supreme Court

1.1 Mental Health Act 1983 and the Mental Health Tribunal

1.1.1 Tribunal applications

- **Capacity to make tribunal application.** *SM v Livewell Southwest CIC* [2020] UKUT 191 (AAC) — (1) This majority decision confirmed that the test for capacity to make a tribunal application stated in the VS case was correct (that the patient must understand that she is being detained against her wishes and that the First-tier Tribunal is a body that will be able to decide whether she should be released). (2) In a dissenting judgment Sarah Johnston DCP stated that the test should be: "Does the patient want to be free to leave?" (3) The

Upper Tribunal decided (again by a majority) that tribunal panel had not erred in striking out the patient's case, and gave detailed procedural guidance, including: (a) if a patient regains capacity then the tribunal should consider inviting the patient to make a fresh application and, having abridged any procedural obligations, proceed to hear the case; (b) anyone can request that the Secretary of State make a reference, including when a patient lacks capacity and wishes to leave hospital: this includes not only the hospital managers and IMHA, but also the tribunal itself, which could adjourn for this purpose instead of immediately striking out the case.

1.1.2   Representation

- **Reviewing appointment of legal representative.** *SB v South London and Maudsley NHS Foundation Trust* [2020] UKUT 33 (AAC) — The tribunal appointed a representative under Tribunal rule 11(7)(b) and later refused to put on record another representative who stated that he was acting on instructions. (1) The initial appointment was unlawful because Form 6b was deficient: the rubric did not mention the 14-day time limit for challenging a delegated decision under Tribunal rule 4. If it had done then the patient's attempt to have a new representative put on record might not have been made too late to be resolved before the hearing. (2) By basing its refusal to review the appointment purely on the appointed solicitor's objection, the tribunal had abdicated its decision-making responsibility and had not given sufficient weight to the presumption of capacity in the face of new evidence of instruction. (3) The decision of the tribunal panel in not discharging the patient was not flawed in any material respect. (4) Neither of the unlawful decisions were set aside as the patient had since been discharged. (5) No damages were awarded as the Upper Tribunal has no power to do so.

1.1.3   Panel composition

- **All-male and all-female panels.** *CB v SSWP* [2020] UKUT 15 (AAC) — (1) It was unlawful of the tribunal to hear the ESA appeal in the applicant's absence; the decision was set aside and the case remitted to a new panel. (2) The judgment contains *obiter* comments about the request for an all-female panel.

- **Direction for all-female panel.** *Re A* [2020] MHLO 14 (FTT) — In this (non-binding) interlocutory decision, a decision to refuse the patient's request for an all-female panel was set aside. The main factor was the overriding objective, in particular ensuring, so far as practicable, that the parties are able to participate fully: the patient's mental state meant that she could only attend the hearing or pre-hearing medical examination if the panel were all female. The judge referred to *obiter* guidance on single-sex panels in a social entitlement case, which referred to "appeals involving sensitive and uniquely female medical conditions" (the other category was "cases raising cultural issues about the giving of evidence"), and noted that the arguments in this case were even more clear cut.

1.1.4 Change in status

- **Change from s3 to s37 during tribunal proceedings.** *GM v Dorset Healthcare University NHS Foundation Trust* [2020] UKUT 152 (AAC) — The First-tier Tribunal had been right to strike out proceedings arising from a s3 reference when the patient was subsequently made subject to a s37 hospital order. It would be contrary to statutory policy if the tribunal were to retain jurisdiction under an application or reference that was made before the date of the hospital order.

- **Change in status – s3 to guardianship.** *AD'A v Cornwall Partnership NHS Foundation Trust* [2020] UKUT 110 (AAC) — When the patient had been transferred from s3 detention to s7 guardianship, the tribunal had been wrong to strike out her case for want of jurisdiction. The tribunal's jurisdiction arose from the s3 application, and none of the subsequent changes (including a new right to apply to tribunal, different tribunal powers, and different parties) affected that jurisdiction.

1.1.5 Coronavirus: CTO hearings

- **Direction for postponement of CTO hearing set aside.** *Re B* [2020] MHLO 18 (FTT) — The initial decision indefinitely to postpone a CTO patient's hearing (in accordance with Mental Health Tribunal, 'Order and directions for all community patients who are subject to a CTO or conditional discharge and who have applied or been referred to the tribunal for the duration of the Pilot Practice Direction' (26/3/20)) was set aside by the First-tier Tribunal.

1.1.6 Coronavirus: remote hearings

- **Video tribunal hearing set aside.** *Re D* [2020] MHLO 51 (FTT) — (1) The decision in this case was set aside because it was not clear whether or not the patient had a reasonable opportunity to hear all the evidence that was given at the hearing: it was not possible to be sure that the patient had a fair hearing. (2) The patient's microphone had been muted for much of the time after giving her evidence at the outset because she "would not stop talking", but this did not amount to exclusion under Tribunal rule 38. [First-tier tribunal decisions are useful but not binding.]

- **Unlawful refusal to adjourn telephone hearing.** *GL v Elysium Healthcare* [2020] UKUT 308 (AAC) — It was wrong for the tribunal to have proceeded with the telephone hearing because: (1) the tribunal had, without investigation, assumed that the patient's flatmate (with whom he was self-isolating to avoid coronavirus) could not overhear; (2) the tribunal had improperly dealt with the patient's anxiety: either it had concluded, without investigation, that the anxiety was without foundation (when he had in fact previously been assaulted because other patients discovered his history), or it had believed the same anxiety would arise at a future hearing (when in fact it arose from the specific circumstances that day); the tribunal should have considered whether his anxiety was genuine and, if so, the impact on his ability to participate; (3) the tribunal had wrongly approached the adjournment request as if the patient had been concerned with the mode of hearing (i.e. telephone) rather than the fear of being overheard that day.

1.1.7   Coronavirus: pre-hearing examinations

- **Remote pre-hearing examinations are practicable.** *Re C* [2020] MHLO 48 (FTT) — (1) A salaried tribunal judge initially refused to allow a pre-hearing examination (PHE) because the coronavirus Pilot Practice Direction states: "During the Covid-19 pandemic it will not be 'practicable' under rule 34 of the 2008 Rules for any PHE examinations to take place, due to the health risk such examinations present." (2) Having treated the rule 46 application for permission to appeal as a rule 6 challenge, a different salaried tribunal judge decided that: (a) the practice direction is subordinate to the rules and overriding objective; (b) in video-enabled hearings with a full panel a PHE is practicable by that means; (c) hearings and PHEs should be conducted remotely as, even if the hospital would allow access, the tribunal will not put its members at risk of contracting or spreading coronavirus; (d) in this case, the PHE would take place by video link on the morning of the hearing. [First-tier Tribunal decisions are not binding.]

- **PHEs: "exceptional" merely refers to an exception to the deeming provision.** *EB v Dorset Healthcare University NHS Foundation Trust* [2020] UKUT 362 (AAC) — The Amended Pilot Practice Direction: Health, Education and Social Care Chamber of the First-Tier Tribunal (Mental Health) (Coronavirus, 14/9/20) (APPD) deems that PHEs are not "practicable" within the meaning of rule 34, unless an authorised judge directs that "in the exceptional circumstances of a particular case it shall be practicable for such a pre-hearing examination to take place, having regard to the overriding objective and any health and safety concerns". EB appealed against a refusal to allow a PHE. The Upper Tribunal held that: (1) the APPD cannot override the terms of the rule, and has to be interpreted, if possible, so as to be valid; (2) circumstances are "exceptional" if, contrary to the deeming provision, a PHE is practicable [in other words, "exceptional" merely refers to an exception to the deeming provision, and the new procedure adds nothing substantive to rule 34]; (3) health and safety concerns would be relevant to practicability even if there had been no pandemic; (4) the overriding objective is also relevant, although it does not allow the tribunal to refuse a PHE for any reason unrelated to practicability (in particular, the amended practice direction can make no change to the existence of the r34 duty, the cases to which it applies, or the purpose of the examination; and the patient's ability to participate in the hearing is not relevant); (5) the availability of the requisite technology for PHEs is relevant to the overriding objective and "[w]here that exists, a PHE need not necessarily have (and may well not have) any material impact on the tribunal's resources" [the decision does not state that the current practice of holding PHEs via CVP and on the hearing day is necessary]; (6) on the facts, the FTT had unlawfully misinterpreted the APPD by considering reasons unrelated to practicability; were EB still detained the decision would have been set aside.

1.1.8 Availability of treatment

- **Lawfulness and availability of treatment.** *PM v Midlands Partnership NHS Foundation Trust* [2020] UKUT 69 (AAC) — The tribunal had been wrong to find that appropriate medical treatment was "available" for a CTO patient for whom the lack of a SOAD certificate meant that two days after the hearing her treatment could not lawfully be given (unless she were to be recalled to hospital and the administration of her depot were to become immediately necessary). This was the case even though the treatment could have been given on the hearing date: the tribunal should look at the whole course of treatment, not merely a snapshot.

1.1.9 Public hearing

- **Public hearing and capacity.** *AR v West London NHS Trust* [2020] UKUT 273 (AAC) — (1) The four factors set out in AH which must be considered in any application for a public hearing under Tribunal rule 38 are merely factors relevant to the ultimate test of whether a public hearing is in the interests of justice. The first factor ("whether it is consistent with the subjective and informed wishes of the patient (assuming that he is competent to make an informed choice")) does not mean that a patient must have capacity in order to be allowed a public hearing, although the wisdom of the patient's wishes is relevant to the application of rule 38. (2) The relevant "matter" for the purposes of assessing capacity is not merely the public hearing application but conduct of the proceedings generally, although lack of capacity in relation to the former entails lack of capacity in relation to the latter. (3) The First-tier Tribunal had restricted its capacity assessment to the decision to apply for a public hearing, and had concluded that "[w]ithout being able to make an informed choice [the patient] cannot have a public hearing", so had erred in relation to both points.

1.1.10 Conditions of discharge

- **Conditional discharge and DOL.** *MC v Cygnet Behavioural Health Ltd* [2020] UKUT 230 (AAC) — (1) Although, following *MM*, the First-tier

Tribunal has no power to impose conditions which would amount to a deprivation of liberty, it does have the power to coordinate its decision with the provision of an authorisation under the MCA, either by "the different hats approach" (the same judge sitting in the COP and the FTT) or "the ducks in a row approach" (adjournment or deferred conditional discharge). (2) This involves no Article 14 discrimination in favour of incapacitous restricted patients as, under SSJ guidance, the equivalent outcome can be reached for capacitous patients by using s17 leave. (3) The FTT had misunderstood the *MM* decision and had been wrong to refuse to defer conditional discharge for a standard authorisation to be put in place. (4) The UT discharged the patient subject to conditions of residence, supervision and compliance with "all aspects of the care package" (surprisingly, as the care package would amount to a deprivation of liberty), to take effect on a specified future date (which s73 does not permit), and with permission to apply to the FTT for variation on a material change in circumstances (presumably only before conditional discharge).

- **Deprivation of liberty during conditional discharge.** *Birmingham City Council v SR* [2019] EWCOP 28 — (1) Both patients supported but lacked capacity in relation to the proposed care plans, which involved deprivation of liberty concurrently with a conditional discharge, and those plans were in their best interests. (2) *Obiter*, the division in the MOJ's post-*MM* guidance (MCA DOL for incapacitous patients whose risk is to themselves, but MHA s17 leave for incapacitous patients whose risk is to others and for capacitous patients) did not withstand scrutiny as it is in patients' best interests to be kept "out of mischief" and therefore out of psychiatric hospital.

- **Condition removed from conditional discharge.** *Re E* [2020] MHLO 52 (FTT) — The tribunal added a condition to the written reasons which was not stated at the hearing: "Abide by the rules applicable to such accommodation in particular to sleep there every night and not to have overnight guests." There had been a clear error of law and the condition was removed: (a) the tribunal had failed to address in its decision why it had made the conditions it made; (b) it was required to provide a brief explanation; (c) it was also required to announce the conditions that the patient was subject to in exact terms, which was crucial given that the patient was being conditionally discharged immediately." [First-tier Tribunal decisions are useful but not binding.]

1.1.11   After-care and community care

- **Private law restitution claim between public bodies.** *Surrey County Council v NHS Lincolnshire CCG* [2020] EWHC 3550 (QB) — The local authority successfully brought a private law claim in restitution against the CCG to recover accommodation and care costs of JD, a young autistic man, on the basis that the CCG had made an error of public law when it twice declined to assess whether JR was eligible for NHS care.

- **Section 117 complaint.** *NHS Guilford and Waverley CCG* (18 007 431a) [2019] MHLO 60 (LGSCO) — Local Government and Social Care Ombudsman decision: "(1) Within one month of my final decision, the Council and CCG will: (a) Write to Miss X and Mr Y, acknowledging the fault identified in this decision and offering meaningful apologies; (b) Jointly pay Mr Y £500 for failure to provide support as outlined on his s117 aftercare plan, delayed care planning, loss of opportunity to re-engage him and distress as a result of poor communication around his care plan and eviction; (c) Jointly pay Miss X £150 for poor complaint handling, stress and inconvenience. (2) Within three months of my final decision, the Council and CCG will ensure that Cherrytrees and all other providers acting on their behalf under s117 review their policies and procedures to ensure compliance with the relevant parts of the Code of Practice: Mental Health Act Code 1983, the Health and Social Care Act 2008 (Regulated Activities) Regulations 2014 and the Care Act 2014, in relation to: (a) Care planning; (b) Daily record keeping; (c) Complaint handling, including ensuring all points are responded to adequately and complainants are properly signposted should they wish to escalate their complaint."

- **Section 117 complaint.** *Milton Keynes CCG* (17 018 823e) [2019] MHLO 61 (LGSCO) — "Whilst the Trust was acting on behalf of the CCG in carrying out the s117 actions, the CCG is ultimately responsible for s.117 provision, along with the Council. ... The CCG, Trust and the Council should, by 23 December: (a) Write to Mrs B apologising for the impact of the fault in relation to not refunding the care fees relating to the supported living placement. (b) Confirm with Mrs B and refund the supported living fees which have not already been reimbursed. Mrs B may need to provide additional information to the organisations about fees paid as part of this. (c) Write to Miss A and Mrs B personally and apologise for the impact the lack of s.117 planning had on both of them individually due to the length of time Miss A went without adequate support. They should also apologise for the uncertainty caused by not knowing whether the incidents outlined above could have been avoided. (d) Pay Miss A £1500 and Mrs B £1000 each in recognition of the impact of the and length of time Miss A had a lack of s.117 support. By 20 February 2020, the Council, CCG and Trust should create an action plan of how they will notify and cooperate with each other to ensure patients are assessed promptly and s.117 care put in place in line with the MHA Code of Practice. This action plan should include a review of progress and the impact of any changes following implementation of the plan."

- **Section status and aftercare.** *Tees, Esk and Wear Valleys NHS Foundation Trust* (19 012 290a) [2020] MHLO 21 (LGSCO) — "Summary: The Ombudsmen find there was fault by a Trust in giving a family incorrect information about a mental health patient's status. When this came to light it caused the patient's wife considerable stress which has not yet been fully addressed. The Ombudsmen also find that fault by a Council meant the patient's wife suffered this stress for too long. The Ombudsmen has recommended small financial payments to act as an acknowledgement of the outstanding injustice."

- **Carer's assessment failures.** *Greater Manchester Mental Health NHS Foundation Trust* (18 018 548a) [2019] MHLO 66 (LGSCO) — LGSCO summary: "The Ombudsmen have upheld Mrs G's complaint about the way her carer's assessments were carried out. We have not found fault with the way the Trust, Council and CCG arranged Mr H's accommodation under s117 of the Mental Health Act or how the Trust communicated with Mrs G and Mr H about this."

- **Complaint not upheld by LGSCO.** *Bassetlaw CCG* (19 006 727a) and *Nottinghamshire Healthcare NHS Foundation Trust* (19 006 727b) [2019] MHLO 67 (LGSCO) — LGSCO summary: "The Ombudsmen found no fault by the Council, Trust or CCG with regards to the care and support they provided to a woman with mental health problems. The Ombudsmen did find fault with a risk assessment the Trust completed. However, we are satisfied this did not have a significant impact on the care the Trust provided."

1.2 Mental Capacity Act 2005 and inherent jurisdiction

1.2.1 Capacity assessment

- **Capacity – DOL.** *Sunderland City Council v AS* [2020] EWCOP 13 — (1) The court decided that a CTO patient lacked capacity in all relevant areas (litigation, residence, care and contact). When giving oral evidence the jointly-instructed psychologist changed her mind on: litigation capacity (initially she thought AS had litigation capacity while not having subject matter capacity), residence (she placed insufficient weight on 'structure and routine', which is an integral part of the information relevant to a decision on residence in supported as opposed to independent living), and fluctuating capacity. The judge noted with approval the approach in NICE guidance on "Decision-making and mental capacity" to people with executive dysfunction. (2) The court authorised the deprivation of liberty (there was a high level of supervision throughout the day and night, in the accommodation and community).

- **Residence and care capacity.** *London Borough of Tower Hamlets v A* [2020] EWCOP 21 — (1) Residence and care decisions are usually considered as individual domains of capacity, in keeping with the MCA's "issue-specific" approach; residence and care decisions involve overlapping information and are not made in separate "silos"; overlap does not mean that a residence decision incorporates a care decision: it is not necessary to make a capacitous decision about care in order to make a capacitous decision about residence. What was required for A to make a capacitous decision about where she lives is a broad understanding of the sort of care which would be provided in each of the two places of residence potentially available to her. Although it was agreed that A lacked capacity to decide how she was cared for, it was decided that she had capacity to decide whether to continue to live in residential care or return to live in her own flat with a care package. (2) Legal Aid would have ended had the DOLS standard authorisation ended: in a postscript the judge decided that, as A had no choice until the home care package was available, "the determination that A lacks capacity to determine the care that she should receive necessarily means that she lacks capacity within the meaning of paragraph 15 of Schedule A1 (that "[t]he relevant person meets the mental capacity requirement if he lacks capacity in relation to the question whether or not he should be accommodated in the relevant hospital or care home for the purpose of being given the relevant care or treatment").

- **Capacity in family case.** *CS v FB* [2020] EWHC 1474 (Fam) — The judge in this international children law case made an interim declaration that the mother lacked capacity to litigate, to enable the Official Solicitor to be appointed as litigation friend and, with the benefit of legal aid, to investigate for final determination the mother's capacity to conduct these proceedings.

- **Expert evidence guidance.** *AMDC v AG* [2020] EWCOP 58 — The court was critical of the jointly-instructed psychiatric reports in this case and provided detailed guidance on how experts' reports on capacity can best assist the court.

1.2.2 Capacity to consent to sexual relations

- **Overlap between different decisions, sex.** *B v A Local Authority* [2019] EWCA Civ 913 — (1) "The important questions on these appeals are as to the factors relevant to making the determinations of capacity which are under challenge and as to the approach to assessment of capacity when the absence of capacity to make a particular decision would conflict with a conclusion that there is capacity to make some other decision." (2) The Court of Appeal also decided on what is necessary to have capacity to consent to sexual relations.

- **Capacity and sexual relations.** *A Local Authority v JB* [2020] EWCA Civ 735 — "The issue arising on this appeal is whether a person, in order to have capacity to decide to have sexual relations with another person, needs to understand that the other person must at all times be consenting to sexual relations."

- **Sexual relations and contact with husband.** *Re SF* [2020] EWCOP 15 — (1) SF lacked capacity in relation to some areas (litigation, care, residence, finances, tenancy, contact with strangers and people who are unfamiliar) but did have capacity to consent to sexual relations and to decide on contact with her husband. The psychiatric evidence was that SF would only have episodic memory ("memory for the personally experienced events of a person's life, with retention of the details of time and situation in which they were acquired") in relation to contact with strangers, but would have semantic memory ("knowledge which is retained irrespective of the circumstances in which it was acquired [deriving] from the 'feeling' around the memory rather than the 'facts' surrounding the memory") in relation to her husband. (2) The court authorised the deprivation of liberty which existed both when living at her home and (on an interim basis until authorised by the placement) when receiving respite care at a residential supported care provision.

1.2.3   Medical and dental treatment

- **Dental treatment – delay.** *Cardiff and Vale University Health Board v P* [2020] EWCOP 8 — "It might seem, from the above account, that some dental assessment was required quickly and now as long ago as November or early December 2019. Plainly, it was. But the application was only made by the Health Board on 20th February 2020. The proposed inspection and/or treatment is not to take place until early March. For anybody who has had toothache, even delay between now and then looks like an eternity. But this young man, it seems, has been suffering, and significantly so, for nearly five months. This is little short of an outrage. It is indefensible. ... An additional complication arose in November when P was taken to the local A&E by his parents with an obvious bruise to his forehead. They believed that his behaviour was so markedly changed that they feared he had some sort of concussion and may have fractured his skull. It is, to my mind, self-evident that there was an urgent medical emergency that should have been investigated within hours or days, but in fact there has, as yet, been no CT scan at all. ... It is, sadly, yet again, a situation in which there has been a fundamental failure to communicate effectively by those responsible for P's care. This message has now been the conclusion of so many reviews, including serious case reviews, that it has become almost trite. There is no point identifying lessons to be learned if they are not, in fact, learned."

- **Haemodialysis under s63 MHA 1983.** *A Healthcare and B NHS Trust v CC* [2020] EWHC 574 (Fam) — "By reason of the above, the Court finds that: (i) The physical condition CC is now in, by which dialysis is critical to keep him alive, is properly described as a manifestation of his mental disorder. There is a very real prospect that if he [were] not mentally ill he would self-care in a way that would have not led to the need for dialysis. Further, CC's refusal of dialysis is very obviously a manifestation of his mental disorder and dialysis treatment is therefore treatment within the scope of section 63 MHA 1983. (ii) CC's capacity to consent to dialysis treatment fluctuates, however his consent is not required in order to be treated, by way of dialysis treatment, under section 63 MHA 1983. (iii) The decision whether it is in CC's best interests to receive dialysis treatment is a matter for CC's responsible clinician (having consulted clinicians attending to his physical health, including the consultant nephrologist), subject to the supervisory jurisdiction of the Court. (iv) Section 58 has no applicability. Section 62 disapplies section 58 in urgent treatment cases such as this where treatment is immediately necessary to save CC's life, to prevent a serious deterioration of his condition, and to alleviate serious suffering. Section 63 is the appropriate course. (v) As section 63 MHA 1983 can be used as authority to provide medical treatment to CC, including by dialysis treatment and by the use of light physical restraint and chemical restraint (if required), it is unnecessary for the court to exercise its discretion and make a contingent declaration pursuant to section 15(1)(c) MCA 2005 that it is lawful to treat CC in accordance with the proposed dialysis treatment plan in the event that he lacks capacity to make a decision regarding dialysis treatment at the relevant time."

- **Force feeding under s63 MHA 1983.** *JK v A Local Health Board* [2019] EWHC 67 (Fam) — "In my view his refusal to contemplate any alternative paths, and his rigid belief that refusing to eat is his only way forward, is a consequence of his autism and as such falls within s.63. The proposed force feeding is therefore certainly capable of being treatment for the manifestation of his mental disorder. However, that does not mean that I by any means accept that force feeding JK would be in his best interests, or critically would be "treatment" that falls within the definition in s.145(4) of the MHA, as being "to alleviate or prevent a worsening of the disorder…". It is apparent that force feeding is a highly intrusive process, which involves sedating the patient whilst the naso-gastric tube is inserted and potentially having to restrain the patient for fairly prolonged periods. This process would be extremely upsetting for any patient, but for JK with his ASD and his aversion to eating in front of other people, the process would be even more traumatic. JK said in oral evidence that he viewed the possibility as abhorrent, and it was clear from that response how incredibly upsetting for all concerned having to go through that process would be. If it came to that stage close consideration would necessarily have to be given to the terms of article 3 ECHR and the caselaw such as *Herczegfalvy v Austria* [1993] 15 EHRR 437 and the test of medical necessity."

- **Withholding life-sustaining treatment from baby.** *Rotherham Metropolitan Borough Council v ZZ* [2020] EWHC 185 (Fam) — "It is impossible not to feel that X's life is one of nothing but suffering. As is set out in the cases above, life itself is precious and there is a very strong presumption in favour of preserving life. But X's life is a truly tragic one and certainly reaches a threshold of intolerability. ... His life expectancy is probably no more than a year on the basis of the literature. ... For all these reasons I am clear that it is not in X's best interests that he should be resuscitated or that he should be given life sustaining treatment."

- **Finely-balanced treatment decision.** *QJ v A Local Authority* [2020] EWCOP 3 — (1) This s21A appeal was adjourned for medical evidence in relation to whether QJ had capacity (a) to decide on whether to receive nutrition and hydration either orally or artificially; (b) to decide more generally on medical treatment; and (c) to decide on admission to hospital. (2) On the day of the hearing QJ had for the first time indicated a willingness to be put on a drip.

Even if QJ were now found to have capacity, the case should still come back before the court because: (a) it may very well be a "finely balanced" decision (and so within Practice Guidance (Court of Protection: Serious Medical Treatment) [2020] EWCOP 2); and, in any event, (b) where there is already an application in relation to the central issue the matter should only be concluded within court proceedings and not left to clinical decisions.

- **Capacity and nutrition/hydration.** *QJ v A Local Authority* [2020] EWCOP 7 — QJ had capacity to decide about nutrition and hydration despite his reluctance to answer certain questions. He was in agreement with the care plan, which included (a) Fortisip; (b) weighing; (c) discharge to a care home; (d) no readmission to hospital if he refuses to accept food or water.

- **Medical treatment delay.** *Sherwood Forest Hospitals NHS Foundation Trust v H* [2020] EWCOP 5 — Noting that the delay in bringing the case to court "may mean that a life is lost that could well have been saved", the judge authorised surgical excision under general anaesthetic of a squamous cell carcinoma on Mrs H's left cheek.

- **Medical treatment.** *Sherwood Forest Hospitals NHS Foundation Trust v H* [2020] EWCOP 6 — In the previous judgment the court had authorised surgical excision of a squamous cell carcinoma on Mrs H's left cheek. By the surgery date its further growth rendered it inoperable. Other treatments, including electro-chemo therapy and palliative radiotherapy under general anaesthetic were under consideration, with a view to putting together a care plan for Mrs H's needs for the remainder of her life. The court would review the care plan because (a) the history of the case required that it be monitored, and (b) Mrs H's daughter had requested this.

- **Treatment despite religious delusions.** *Sherwood Forest Hospitals NHS Foundation Trust v C* [2020] EWCOP 10 — (1) Having previously undergone two hysteroscopies, and initially consented to removal of her ovaries and fallopian tubes, C disengaged, expressed religious views (such as that only God could cure her cancer), and was assessed as lacking capacity. The judge decided that "she clearly lacked capacity and her rejection of the treatment, which is clinically so manifestly in her best interests, is predicated on a delusional belief structure which manifests itself in the language of religion". (2) The delay in this case, which was attributable to the treating clinicians not initially knowing C had paranoid schizophrenia, and their reluctance to contemplate coercion, should not have happened and likely stressed C and her family, but had not led to neglect of the cancer.

- **Competence/capacity and puberty blockers.** *Bell v Tavistock And Portman NHS Foundation Trust* [2020] EWHC 3274 (Admin) — (1) The relevant information that a child would have to understand, retain and weigh up in order to have the requisite competence in relation to puberty blockers, would be as follows: (i) the immediate consequences of the treatment in physical and psychological terms; (ii) the fact that the vast majority of patients taking puberty blockers go on to cross-sex hormones and therefore that he or she is on a pathway to much greater medical interventions; (iii) the relationship between taking cross-sex hormones and subsequent surgery, with the implications of such surgery; (iv) the fact that cross-sex hormones may well lead to a loss of fertility; (v) the impact of cross-sex hormones on sexual function; (vi) the impact that taking this step on this treatment pathway may have on future and life-long relationships; (vii) the unknown physical consequences of taking PBs; and (viii) the fact that the evidence base for this treatment is as yet highly uncertain. (2) *Gillick* competence is treatment- and person-specific but the court gave clear guidance that it is highly unlikely that a child aged 13 or under, and very doubtful that a child aged 14 or 15, would ever be *Gillick* competent to give consent to being treated with puberty blockers. (3) There is a presumption that young people aged 16 or over have capacity to consent but, given the long-term and potentially irreversible consequences and the experimental nature of the treatment, clinicians may well consider that it is not appropriate to move to treatment such as puberty blockers or cross-sex hormones without the involvement of the court, and it would be appropriate to involve the court when there may be any doubt about long-term best interests.

- **Death and religion.** *JB v University Hospitals Plymouth NHS Trust* [2020] EWCA Civ 1772 — The COP had decided that it was in RS's best interests not to receive life-sustaining treatment, including artificial ventilation, nutrition and fluids. On appeal, his niece argued that the decision was unjust because of serious procedural error in that it was taken with an insufficient degree of inquiry into how RS would have wanted to be treated against the backdrop of the tenets of his Roman Catholic faith (and also that the judge breached natural justice and Article 6 by prohibiting cross-examination of RS's wife on the grounds that she was distressed and/or by permitting her to communicate additional evidence by a confidential letter to the judge which was not disclosed to the parties). Permission to appeal was not granted.

1.2.4   Forced abortion

- **Abortion.** *An NHS Foundation Trust v AB* [2019] EWCOP 26 — "This is an application by the NHS Trust for an order in respect of a 24 year old woman AB who is 22 weeks pregnant and, who the Trust say lacks capacity and in whose best interests it is said to have a termination of pregnancy. ... I would like to record my unhappiness about the lateness of this application. AB is now estimated to be 22 weeks pregnant and therefore the cut-off date under the Abortion Act 1967 of 24 weeks is imminent. ... I am acutely conscious of the fact that for the state to order someone to have a termination, where it appears that they do not want it, is immensely intrusive and certainly interferes with her Article 8 rights. ... In my view the balance in terms of AB's best interests lies in her having the termination."

- **Abortion.** *Re AB (Termination of Pregnancy)* [2019] EWCA Civ 1215 — "The requirement is for the court to consider both wishes and feelings. The judge placed emphasis on the fact that AB's wishes were not clear and were not clearly expressed. She was entitled to do that but the fact remains that AB's feelings were, as for any person, learning disabled or not, uniquely her own and are not open to the same critique based upon cognitive or expressive ability. AB's feelings were important and should have been factored into the balancing exercise alongside consideration of her wishes. ... [I]n my judgement, she clearly gave inadequate weight to the non-medical factors in the case, while the views expressed by the doctors were necessarily significantly predicated upon imponderables. In the end, the evidence taken as a whole was simply not sufficient to justify the profound invasion of AB's rights represented by the non-consensual termination of this advanced pregnancy."

1.2.5   Inherent jurisdiction: adults

- **Inherent jurisdiction.** *Mazhar v Birmingham Community Healthcare Foundation NHS Trust* [2020] EWCA Civ 1377 — Mr Mazhar was removed from his home to hospital without warning by police and paramedics in the middle of the night under the High Court's inherent jurisdiction on the basis of an out-of-hours application. (1) The Trust's application for, and the granting of, the order for which there was no proper evidence and without giving Mr Mazhar the opportunity to be heard amounted to a clear breach of his Article 6 rights and was a flagrant denial of justice. (2) It was unnecessary to decide whether the inherent jurisdiction extends to the making of an order that has the effect of depriving a vulnerable adult of liberty provided the provisions of Article 5 are met. (3) The President of Family Division was invited to consider whether fresh guidance should be given to practitioners and judges about applications of this sort, and the court set out a list of seven clear lessons to be learnt.

- **Inherent jurisdiction – dispensing with service.** *A Local Authority v B* [2020] EWHC 2741 (Fam) — It was proper to dispense with service of proceedings on B's father in relation to inherent jurisdiction proceedings seeking a declaration authorising the deprivation of B's liberty at a community therapeutic placement following discharge from section 2 detention in hospital.

1.2.6   Inherent jurisdiction: children

- **Inherent jurisdiction and DOL.** *Lancashire County Council v G* [2020] EWHC 2828 (Fam) — A 16-year-old girl was inappropriately placed on an adult mental health ward, there was no secure placement or regulated non-secure placement was available in the UK, the only placement was an unregulated placement that was not prepared to apply to OFSTED for registration, and the alternative was discharge with nowhere to go and a very high risk of fatal self-harm. The judge authorised deprivation of liberty at the unauthorised placement but noted grave reservations about whether the court was really exercising its welfare jurisdiction or simply being forced by mere circumstance to make an order irrespective of welfare considerations. The judge directed the judgment be sent to the Children's Commissioner for England, the Secretary of State for Education, the Chair of the Residential Care Leadership Board, the Minister for Children, the Chief Social Worker, OFSTED and SWCU.

- **Shortage of secure accommodation.** Ellen Lloyd, 'Case Summary: Lancashire CC v G (2020) EWHC 2828' (Bevan Brittan, 9/12/20) — This article discusses the court's approach to deprivation of liberty of children in unregulated non-secure accommodation. Headings include: (1) Practical impact; (2) What is the difference between secure and non-secure accommodation, regulated and unregulated?; (3) What should a Court consider when determining an application for a secure accommodation order?; (4) What happens if there is no secure accommodation available?

- **DOL of child at unregulated placement.** *Lancashire County Council v G (No 2)* [2020] EWHC 3124 (Fam) — (1) The judge concluded that "once again with deep reservations, I [remain] satisfied on balance that it is in G's best interests to authorise the deprivation of her liberty in her current placement notwithstanding that the placement is plainly sub-optimal from the perspective of meeting G's identified and highly complex welfare needs and is an unregulated placement". (2) The following observations by the Children's Commissioner in a briefing paper entitled "The children who no-one knows what to do with" (published in November 2020 after the previous judgment in this case) were noted: (a) no work is being done to forecast and co-ordinate provision of secure accommodation and regulated placements in order to match need; (b) there are some 200 children awaiting a place in secure accommodation; (c) during 2018/2019 12,800 children spent some time accommodated in unregulated placements with no regulatory oversight by OFSTED.

- **DOL of child at unregulated placement.** *Lancashire County Council v G (No 3)* [2020] EWHC 3280 (Fam) — (1) The judge authorised deprivation of liberty at a sub-optimal placement as there was no other option but discharge into the community where she would almost certainly cause herself possibly fatal harm. (2) The judge noted the following points from the Children's Commissioner's November 2020 report entitled "Who are they? Where are they? 2020 – Children Locked

Up": "(i) There continues to be a group of children who are being deprived of their liberty in settings which are not deemed appropriate. These children are in need of a placement that can manage the high level of risk that they present whilst holding them securely but there are no such placements available. (ii) There is no official data on the numbers of children who find themselves in this position but it would appear that at there are a significant number of extremely vulnerable children who professionals have decided are in need of a bed in a secure accommodation unit but who are instead are placed in unregulated placement. (iii) There is evidence that, with high numbers of children waiting to be placed, perverse incentives exist for placements to take the children who pose the least risk rather than the children who have the most need. (iv) There are a group of children who fall between the gaps of all placement settings, children for whom secure accommodation is not available or appropriate but who also do not meet the criteria under the Mental Health Act 1983 for admission to a mental health ward."

- **Secure accommodation and inherent jurisdiction.** *A City Council v LS* [2019] EWHC 1384 (Fam) — "Does the High Court have power under its inherent jurisdiction, upon the application of a local authority, to authorise the placement in secure accommodation of a 17-year-old child who is not looked after by that local authority within the meaning of s 22(1) of the Children Act 1989, whose parent objects to that course of action, but who is demonstrably at grave risk of serious, and possibly fatal harm. I am satisfied that the answer is 'no'."

- **Inherent jurisdiction and DOL.** *Hertfordshire CC v K* [2020] EWHC 139 (Fam) — "In this matter, the question before the court is whether it should grant a deprivation of liberty order (hereafter a DOL order) under the inherent jurisdiction of the High Court in respect of AK, born in 2003 and now aged 16."

1.2.7   Contingent and interim declarations

- **Contingent/anticipatory declarations – MCA/inherent jurisdiction – Caesarean section.** *Guy's and St Thomas' NHS Foundation Trust v R* [2020] EWCOP 4 — R had capacity to make decisions as to her ante-natal and obstetric care but there was a risk that she would lose capacity during labour and refuse a Caesarean section. (1) MCA 2005 s16 (Powers to make decisions and appoint deputies: general) applies only to those who currently lack capacity. (2) MCA 2005 s15 (Power to make declarations) is not so limited and so can authorise contingent declarations. (3) Deprivation of liberty cannot be authorised by s15 but the inherent jurisdiction may be utilised to fill that lacuna which would otherwise render the s15 power nugatory.

- **Interim declarations under s48 MCA 2005.** *DA v DJ* [2017] EWHC 3904 (Fam) — In this case Parker J followed the approach of HHJ Marshall QC in

Re F [2009] EWHC B30 (Fam) rather than the approach of Hayden J in *Wandsworth LBC v A McC* [2017] EWHC 2435 (Fam) in relation to the correct approach to the threshold test for making an interim order under MCA 2005 s48 (which requires that there is "reason to believe that P lacks capacity in relation to the matter"). There is no need for the purpose and extent of the capacity assessment to be explained to the person concerned, and the evidence does not need to go so far as to rebut the presumption of capacity.

1.2.8   Litigation friends

- **Protected party – litigation friend.** *Hinduja v Hinduja* [2020] EWHC 1533 (Ch) — (1) Medical evidence on capacity to conduct proceedings is not required under the CPR, and in this case to require it would not be necessary or in accordance with the overriding objective. The court decided that SP was a protected party. (2) The defendants argued that the proposed litigation friend failed both limbs of the relevant test (ability fairly and competently to conduct proceedings and having no adverse interest). Having considered the tests (including noting that "[w]hether the existence of a financial interest on the part of the litigation friend should debar [her] from acting will depend on the nature of the interest, and whether it is in fact adverse or whether it otherwise prevents the litigation friend conducting the proceedings fairly and competently on the protected party's behalf") the court made the appointment sought.

- **Appointeeship, independent appeals, litigation friends.** *RH v SSWP* [2018] UKUT 48 (AAC) — AACR headnote: "Appointment to act – whether claimant with appointee precluded from bringing an appeal independently – whether First-tier Tribunal having power to appoint a litigation friend"

- **EAT capacity and litigation friend.** *Stott v Leadec Ltd* [2020] UKEAT 263/19 — The Employment Appeal Tribunal adjourned for a medical report on litigation capacity and commented on the continuing lack of rules rules containing clearly defined powers in relation to proceedings involving protected parties (as defined in Part 21 of the CPR) in employment tribunals and in the EAT.

1.2.9   Foreign orders

- **Foreign representative powers.** *Re GED* [2019] EWCOP 52 — "[T]hree broad issues have been identified: (1) Is a foreign power of attorney capable of constituting a 'protective measure'? (2) Is there a capacity threshold to the Court's jurisdiction? (3) Where there is a valid and operable foreign power of attorney in place, is the jurisdiction of the Court of Protection under section 16 of the Mental Capacity Act 2005 limited?"

- **Recognition of foreign protective measure.** *Health Service Executive of Ireland v Moorgate* [2020] EWCOP 12 — (1) The necessary criteria were met for the recognition and enforcement of protective measures contained in an order made by the Southern Irish High Court which authorised the patient's transfer from a London hospital to a specialist hospital in Leeds. (2) An appendix entitled "Domestic regimes applicable to SM and those in her position" contains the following headings: (a) Application of the MHA; (b) Hospital admission under the MHA; (c) Treatment under the MHA; (d) Representation and support; (e) Challenging detention; (f) Removal of alien patients; (g) Mental Capacity Act 2005 (excluding the provisions of Schedule 3); (h) Inherent jurisdiction of the High Court; (i) Comparison of protections under MHA and under Schedule 3.

- **Habitual residence.** *Re QD* [2019] EWCOP 56 — QD, who had dementia, was living in Spain with his second wife when adult children from his first marriage flew him to England by stealth. The children unsuccessfully argued that: (a) he was now habitually resident in England, so the MCA applied in the usual way; (b) removal was justified under the common law doctrine of necessity; (c) jurisdiction was established on grounds of urgency; (d) even if QD were habitually resident in Spain, orders could be made under the inherent jurisdiction. The judge therefore made a protective measures order under sch 3 MCA 2005 pending a determination by the national authorities in Spain on what should happen next.

  - **Habitual residence.** *Re QD (No.2)* [2020] EWCOP 14 — A legal deadlock had arisen: (a) the English court did not have primary jurisdiction, as QD was habitually resident in Spain; (b) the Spanish court would not exercise its jurisdiction unless QD were in Spain; (c) there was no obligation to return QD there. The coronavirus travel bans meant an "urgent" decision under MCA 2005 sch 3 that he be returned could not be made, so the decision was adjourned for 3-4 months.

1.2.10 Deputyship and LPA

- **Deputies and litigation.** *Re ACC* [2020] EWCOP 9 — This case concerned whether, and in what circumstances, a property and affairs deputy can recover from the protected person's assets costs which have been or are likely to be incurred in legal proceedings. The applicant deputies from Irwin Mitchell wanted to know when a professional deputy may instruct a legal firm with which it is associated and recover the costs from P. The court gave detailed guidance, including a summary of conclusions in an appendix.

- **Care, and deputyship.** *Essex County Council v CVF* [2020] EWCOP 65 — The court dealt with three issues: (1) the amount of care and support CVF needed; (2) whether the local authority should replace CVF's mother, JF, as property and affairs deputy (yes); (3) whether JF should be appointed as personal welfare deputy (no).

- **Whether to register LPAs.** *Re KC: LCR v SC* [2020] EWCOP 62 — (1) The three-stage test in *Re J* [2010] MHLO 167 (COP) for revocation of an LPA was applied to LPA registration in this case: the LPAs were not registered as the acrimonious relationship among the donees would prevent them from acting in KC's best interests. (2) a panel deputy for property and affairs was appointed, but no personal welfare deputy.

1.2.11 Miscellaneous capacity cases

- **Court of Protection permission.** *Re D: A v B* [2020] EWCOP 1 — (1) The appropriate threshold for permission under MCA 2005 s50 is the same as that applicable in the field of judicial review: to gain permission the claimant or applicant has to demonstrate a good arguable case. (2) In the current case, the decision to be made was "whether a good arguable case has been shown that it is in [D's] best interests for there to be a full welfare investigation of the current contact arrangements" and the judge's conclusion was: "I cannot say that I am satisfied that the mother has shown a good arguable case that a substantive application would succeed if permission were granted."

- **DOL and common law.** *R (Jalloh) v SSHD* [2020] UKSC 4 — "The right to physical liberty was highly prized and protected by the common law long before the United Kingdom became party to the European Convention on Human Rights. A person who was unlawfully imprisoned could, and can, secure his release through the writ of habeas corpus. He could, and can, also secure damages for the tort of false imprisonment. This case is about the meaning of imprisonment at common law and whether it should, or should not, now be aligned with the concept of deprivation of liberty in article 5 of the ECHR."

- **FMPOs and capacity.** *Re K (Forced Marriage: Passport Order)* [2020] EWCA Civ 190 — (1) The Family Court the court has jurisdiction to make a Forced Marriage Protection Order to protect an adult who does not lack mental capacity (and the statistics demonstrate that the courts regularly make FMPOs to protect capacitous adults). (2) An open-ended passport order or travel ban should only be imposed in the most exceptional of cases and where the court can look sufficiently far into the future to be satisfied that highly restrictive orders of that nature will be required indefinitely.

- **Disclosure of documents.** *Re Z* [2019] EWCOP 55 — "This is an application by JK, who is a son of Z, for the disclosure to him of certain documents which have been filed by the other parties in the course of these proceedings and prior to the making of the [court's] order."

- **Testamentary capacity.** *Clitheroe v Bond* [2020] EWHC 1185 (Ch) — "This is a bitter family dispute between the Claimant brother and Defendant sister as to whether their mother, the deceased, had testamentary capacity to make each of her two wills and in addition or in the alternative whether either or both wills resulted from fraudulent calumny."

1.3 Criminal law

- **Diminished responsibility sentencing.** *R v Rodi* [2020] EWCA Crim 330 — Unsuccessful appeal against s45A and 10-year sentence, in which the November 2018 sentencing guidelines for diminished responsibility manslaughter were applied.

- **Successful s45A appeal.** *R v Westwood* [2020] EWCA Crim 598 — "In the circumstances of this case there was a sound reason for departing from the need to impose a sentence with a "penal element". In view of the low level of the appellant's "retained responsibility", the likelihood that for the rest of his life he will need psychiatric treatment and supervision that can most effectively be provided through orders under sections 37 and 41 of the Mental Health Act, and the likely advantages in this case of the regime for and on his release under such orders when compared to an order under section 45A, we consider that that is the right disposal here."

- **Insanity legislation and foreign criminals.** *SSHD v MZ* [2020] UKUT 225 (IAC) — A person sentenced to a hospital order following a finding under CPIA 1964 s5(1)(b) that he "is under a disability and that he did the act or made the omission charged against him" is not subject to s117C Nationality, Immigration and Asylum Act 2002 ("Article 8: additional considerations in cases involving foreign criminals") or paragraphs A398-399 (also concerning deportation of foreign criminals) of the Immigration Rules.

- **Sentencing and mental health.** *R v PS* [2019] EWCA Crim 2286 — "These three cases, otherwise unconnected, raise issues about proper approach to sentencing offenders who suffer from autism or other mental health conditions or disorders."

- **Appeal against IPP.** *R v Stredwick* [2020] EWCA Crim 650 — "In this appeal the appellant invites the court to quash the sentence of imprisonment for public protection imposed in 2008 and make an order pursuant to section 37 of the Mental Health Act 1983 ("the 1983 Act") for his admission or continued detention at Ty Gwyn Hall Hospital, Abergavenny. The appellant also invites the court to make an accompanying Restriction Order without limit of time under section 41 of the 1983 Act. The Crown does not oppose this appeal, nor the orders sought."

- **Restricted hospital order instead of life sentence.** *R v Cleland* [2020] EWCA Crim 906 — Life sentence with 7-year minimum term quashed and substituted with s37/41 restricted hospital order.

- **Hybrid order or restricted hospital order.** *R v Nelson* [2020] EWCA Crim 1615 — The Court of Appeal considered the differences between a hybrid order (s45A) and a restricted hospital order (s37/41), the guidance from caselaw and the Sentencing Council's Guideline on "Sentencing offenders with mental disorders, developmental disorders or neurological impairment" which came into effect on 1/10/20.

1.4 Inquests

- **Inquest and DOLS.** *R (Maguire) v HM Senior Coroner for Blackpool and Fylde* [2020] EWCA Civ 738 — "The issue for determination in this appeal is whether the circumstances surrounding the death of Jacqueline Maguire (known as Jackie) required the coroner to allow the jury at her inquest to return an expanded conclusion in accordance with section 5(2) of the Coroners and Justice Act 2009. ... Jackie was subject to a standard authorisation granted by Blackpool Council pursuant to the Deprivation of Liberty Safeguards set out in Schedule A1 to the Mental Capacity Act 2005. ... Jackie's circumstances were not analogous with a psychiatric patient who is in hospital to guard against the risk of suicide. She was accommodated by United Response to provide a home in which she could be looked after by carers, because she was unable to look after herself and it was not possible for her to live with her family. She was not there for medical treatment. If she needed medical treatment it was sought, in the usual way, from the NHS. Her position would not have been different had she been able to continue to live with her family with social services input and been subject to an authorisation from the Court of Protection in respect of her deprivation of liberty whilst in their care."

- **Inquest determination and findings quashed.** *Rushbrooke v HM Coroner for West London* [2020] EWHC 1612 (Admin) — The applicant, who had been the deceased's Relevant Person's Representative under a DOLS authorisation successfully argued for the inquest's determination and findings to be quashed.

- **Article 2 inquests and community patients.** *R (Lee) v HM Assistant Coroner for Sunderland* [2019] EWHC 3227 (Admin) — The coroner had decided that Article 2 was not engaged in this case, which involved the death of a community patient who was not subject to the MHA. (1) In relation to the operational duty, the coroner's decision had focussed almost exclusively on the question of responsibility rather than the "threefold factors of assumed responsibility, vulnerability and risk" set out in the *Rabone* case. The matter was remitted to the coroner for reconsideration. (2) The grounds which related to systemic failures were unarguable.

  - **Article 2 inquests and community patients.** *Re Lee* [2019] MHLO 73 (Coroner) — The coroner, following the Administrative Court decision that she had failed properly to address the Article 2 operational duty as set out in the *Rabone* case, in this decision sets out reasons for concluding that (a) the operational duty was neither engaged nor breached.

1.5   Medical records

- **Disclosure of patient's medical information.** *ABC v St George's Healthcare NHS Trust* [2020] EWHC 455 (QB) — "By this claim brought against three NHS trusts, the claimant contends that the defendants breached a duty of care owed to her and/or acted contrary to her rights under Article 8 of the European Convention on Human Rights in failing to alert her to the risk that she had inherited the gene for Huntington's disease in time for her to terminate her pregnancy."

- **Access to records of deceased patient.** *Re AB* [2020] EWHC 691 (Fam) — The Access to Health Records Act 1990 states that "[a]n application for access to a health record, or to any part of a health record, may be made to the holder of the record by ... where the patient has died, the patient's personal representative and any person who may have a claim arising out of the patient's death" but limits this as follows: "access shall not be given ... to any part of the record which, in the opinion of the holder of the record, would disclose information which is not relevant to any claim which may arise out of the patient's death." The two categories are disjunctive and the reference to "a claim arising out of the patient's death" is expressly tied to the second, and not to a personal representative.

1.6   Parole Board

- **Parole Board representation for those lacking capacity.** *R (EG) v Parole Board* [2020] EWHC 1457 (Admin) — (1) The Parole Board Rules 2019 introduced a power to appoint a representative "where the prisoner lacks the capacity to appoint a representative and the panel chair or duty member believes that it is in the prisoner's best interests for the prisoner to be represented". In the absence of anything similar to the accreditation system operating in the MHT (and the LAA's pragmatic approach to the regulation preventing providers from making an application for Legal Aid) a solicitor cannot "assume the dual role of legal representative and litigation friend" and so this appointment power cannot be exercised. (2) The 2019 rules, although silent on the matter, allow for the appointment of a litigation friend because: (a) "other representative" in the expression "solicitor, barrister or other representative" includes litigation friend; and, if that is wrong, (b) as with the 2016 rules, it is allowed when necessary under the general power to make directions. (3) In the absence of an accreditation scheme or other litigation friend, the prisoner needed the Official Solicitor to act if his parole review was to progress; (*obiter*) the OS has the statutory power to act in Parole Board proceedings. (4) The judge limited her decision to issues concerning EG individually, and criticised counsel for EG and the EHRC for continuing the trend in public law litigation of grounds of challenge evolving during proceedings in a way which lacked procedural rigour (in this case, by raising wider issues including the identification and assessment of non-capacitous prisoners and the Public Sector Equality Duty).

- **Reconsideration of Parole Board decision.** *Joseph, Application for Reconsideration by* [2019] PBRA 43 — Unsuccessful application by prisoner with mental health background for reconsideration on basis of irrationality and procedural unfairness of Parole Board oral hearing panel's decision not to direct release on licence.

1.7 Miscellaneous cases

- **Non-application of forfeiture rule.** *Re W* [2020] UKUT 155 (AAC) — The forfeiture rule ("the rule of public policy which in certain circumstances precludes a person who has unlawfully killed another from acquiring a benefit in consequence of the killing") can be modified in the interests of justice but not following a conviction for murder. The Secretary of State initially argued that W had been convicted of murder. The Crown Court had found that, in relation to his wife's killing, W was unfit to plead but had done the act. The Upper Tribunal equated this with a finding of not guilty by reason of insanity, which for forfeiture rule purposes amounts to an acquittal, so there was no conviction and the forfeiture rule did not apply.

- **Ex turpi causa.** *Henderson v Dorset Healthcare University NHS Foundation Trust* [2020] UKSC 43 — The respondent admitted negligently failing to return the appellant to hospital on the basis of her manifest psychotic state, which led to her stabbing her mother to death. The Supreme Court held that the previous case of *Gray v Thames Trains Ltd* [2009] UKHL 33 could not be distinguished, and should not be departed from, and that therefore the claim was barred by the doctrine of *ex turpi causa non oritur actio* (illegality).

- **ECHR and subordinate legislation.** *RR v SSWP* [2019] UKSC 52 — (1) There is nothing unconstitutional about a public authority, court or tribunal disapplying a provision of subordinate legislation which would otherwise result in their acting incompatibly with a Convention right, where this is necessary in order to comply with the Human Rights Act 1998. (2) On the facts of this case, the public authority should disobey Regulation B13 of the Housing Benefit Regulations 2006 and retrospectively apply the Supreme Court's decision in *R (Carmichael) v SSWP* [2016] UKSC 58 that the "bedroom tax" was an unjustified discrimination on the ground of disability where there was a transparent medical need for an additional bedroom.

- **Vulnerable witnesses.** *Re C (Female Genital Mutilation and Forced Marriage: Fact Finding)* [2019] EWHC 3449 (Fam) — Paragraphs 14-18 deal with "Assessing the Evidence of Vulnerable Witnesses", including the following: "Despite my very considerable sympathy for witnesses with significant vulnerabilities such as the mother in this case, my clear view is that there is one standard of proof which applies without modification irrespective of the characteristics of witnesses, including vulnerable witnesses to whom Part 3A and PD3AA apply. I observe that many vulnerable witnesses are just as likely as anyone else either to tell the truth or to lie deliberately or misunderstand events. It would be unfair and discriminatory to discount a witness's evidence because of their inherent vulnerabilities (including mental and cognitive disabilities) and it would be equally wrong in principle not to apply a rigorous analysis to a witness's evidence merely because they suffer from mental, cognitive or emotional difficulties. To do otherwise would, in effect, attenuate the standard of proof when applied to witnesses of fact with such vulnerabilities. ... Having said that, I offer the following observations, none of them particularly novel, which might assist in assessing the evidence of vulnerable witnesses, particularly those with learning disabilities. First, it is simplistic to conclude that the evidence of such a witness is inherently unreliable. Second, it is probably unfair to expect the same degree of verbal fluency and articulacy which one might expect in a witness without those problems. Third, it is important not to evaluate the evidence of such a witness on the basis of intuition which may or may not be unconsciously biased. Finally, it is important to take into account and make appropriate allowances for that witness's disability or vulnerability, assisted by any expert or other evidence available."

- **Charitable status of foundation trusts.** *Derby Teaching Hospitals NHS Foundation Trust v Derby City Council* [2019] EWHC 3436 (Ch) — Seventeen NHS foundation trusts argued that, as foundation trusts, they were entitled under s43(5) Local Government Finance Act 1988 to the four-fifths reduction in non-domestic rates because they were charities and the relevant properties were wholly or mainly used for charitable purposes. The High Court answered the preliminary question "Whether the Lead Claimant is a charity for the purposes of section 43(6) of the Local Government Finance Act 1988?" in the negative.

- **Lay advocates in public law family proceedings.** *Re C (Lay Advocates)* [2019] EWHC 3738 (Fam) — "In my judgment that there is no material difference between the services provided by an interpreter, an intermediary or a lay advocate insofar as they each enable and support parties and witnesses to communicate and understand these proceedings. HMCTS routinely pay for the services of interpreters and intermediaries, I cannot see any principled reason why it should not also pay for the services of lay advocates in an appropriate case. ... Accordingly, I will appoint a lay advocate for the mother and a lay advocate for the father. They cost £30 per hour which I consider to be entirely reasonable. I have assessed the likely number of hours of work on this for the lay advocates to be 50 hours."

- **Audio recording of neuropsychological testing.** *MacDonald v Burton* [2020] EWHC 906 (QB) — (1) The defendant was allowed to carry its neuropsychological examination of the claimant without being subjected to any kind of recording of that examination: a level playing field could not be achieved where the claimant had not recorded the examination and testing by his own expert but where the examination testing by the defendant's expert was so recorded. (2) The judge discussed the question of any privilege which may exist in any recordings that are made. (3) The judge hoped that the forthcoming British Psychological Association guidance would recognise the competing interests and would not merely state that psychological examinations and testing should never be recorded.

2 Legislation

All 2020 legislation (including any added since this booklet was published) can be browsed on the database at: www.mhlo.uk/ch.

2.1 Electronic forms

- **Legislation.** Mental Health (Hospital, Guardianship and Treatment) (England) (Amendment) Regulations 2020 — These Regulations amend Mental Health (Hospital, Guardianship and Treatment) (England) Regulations 2008 to provide for the service of documents by electronic communication.

2.2 Coronavirus

- **Legislation.** Coronavirus Act 2020 — This Act, among other things, amends the MHA 1983 in light of the coronavirus pandemic. The Act is in force on 25/3/20, although s10 and schedules 8-11 (amendments to the MHA and NI/Scottish equivalents) will commence on a date to be specified in regulations. The paragraphs of schedule 8 relating to "Constitution and proceedings of the Mental Health Review Tribunal for Wales" came into force on 27/3/20.

  - **Progress of Coronavirus Bill in Parliament.** Parliament website, 'Coronavirus Bill 2019-21' — This web page contains the links to the full text of the Bill as introduced on 19/3/20, explanatory notes, and other documents.

  - **Information about Coronavirus Bill.** DHSC, 'Coronavirus bill: what it will do' (18/3/20) — "The Department of Health and Social Care (DHSC) has identified that to effectively manage a coronavirus outbreak in the UK, we need to introduce new fast-tracked legislation. This will provide us with the legal measures to be able to implement our phased response. This paper sets out, subject to final approvals, the elements of the new legislation and why they are needed." It will involve changes to mental health law.

  - **Description of MHA changes in Coronavirus Bill.** Simon Burrows, 'Amendments to the Mental Health Act 1983 proposed in the Coronavirus Bill 2020 as originally submitted to Parliament' (Law in the Time of Corona Blog, 23/3/20) — This article contains information under the following headings: (1) Introduction; (2) The Coronavirus Bill – its purpose; (3) The process of detention: sections 2, 3, 4 and 5 MHA; (4) Patients involved in the criminal justice process; (5) Administration of medication without consent; (6) Police powers: places of safety; (7)

Transitional Provisions; (8) Deprivation of liberty under the Mental Capacity Act?; (9) Concluding remarks.

- **Summary of Coronavirus Act 2000.** Hill Dickinson LLP, 'Coronavirus Act – key facts' (26/3/20) — This detailed summary of the Coronavirus Act 2020 contains the following headings: (1) Emergency registration of health and social care professionals; (2) Suspension of duties to undertake assessments of need/discharge of patients from hospital; (3) Deaths and inquests; (4) Indemnity for health service activity; (5) Powers in relation to potentially infectious persons; (6) Children; (7) Offences; (8) Impact on NHS employers; (9) Emergency volunteering leave; (10) Statutory sick pay; (11) Changes to the Mental Health Act 1983: (a) Applications for detention under section 2 and section 3; (b) Holding powers; (c) Treatment – administration of medicine to persons liable to detention in hospital; (d) Detention in place of safety; (e) Patients concerned with the criminal justice system.

- **Coronavirus public health restrictions.** Alex Ruck Keene, 'Public health restrictions and capacity' (Mental Capacity Law and Policy, 29/3/20) — This blog post discusses the public health powers within the Coronavirus Act 2020. The material relating to the initial coronavirus restrictions (which were substantially amended) has been moved to a separate article.

- **Coronavirus mental health law changes.** Hannah Taylor, 'Coronavirus Act 2020 – Changes for Mental Health' (Bevan Brittan, 1/4/20) — This web page sets out the proposed changes to the MHA in table format. It then gives some information under the following headings: (1) What about potentially infectious persons in the mental health context? (2) Patients who refuse to self-isolate; (3) How should public authorities be preparing for the changes? (a) Communication; (b) Environmental preparation; (c) Informing staff; (d) Training and guidance; (e) Alternative arrangements; (f) Statutory forms.

- **Legislation.** Coronavirus Act 2020 (Commencement No 1) (Wales) Regulations 2020 — This brings into force: (1) paragraphs 11, 12 and 13 of schedule 8, removing the need for three panel members and making other changes to MHRT for Wales procedure, on 27/3/20; (2) some of schedule 12, removing and modifying certain duties under the Social Services and Well-being (Wales) Act 2014, on 1/4/20.

- **Legislation.** Coronavirus Act 2020 (Expiry of Mental Health Provisions) (England and Wales) Regulations 2020 — This legislation expires most of the mental health amendments in sch 8 Coronavirus Act 2020 in relation to England, and some in relation to Wales. None of the expired provisions had commenced. Some other amendments will continue in Wales (mainly those relating to the MHRT) and transitional provisions will remain in force in both countries.

- **Legislation.** Tribunal Procedure (Coronavirus) (Amendment) Rules 2020 — Rule 2 amends the MHT's rules: (1) new power in new rule 5A to dispose of proceedings without hearing if the matter is urgent, it is not reasonably practicable to hold a hearing (including a remote hearing) and it is in the interests of justice to do so. (2) section 2 hearings to start within 10 days rather than 7 days, with an explicit power to ignore this deadline if the tribunal considers it "not reasonably practicable". In force 10/4/20. These rules will expire on the same day as section 55(b) of the Coronavirus Act 2020 (public participation in proceedings conducted by video or audio). (3) A further change, relating to public/private hearings, is inserted into the part of the HESC rules which do not apply to mental health cases.

- **Legislation.** Health Protection (Coronavirus) Regulations 2020 — The explanatory note states: "These Regulations supplement the health protection regime found in Part 2A of the Public Health (Control of Disease) Act 1984 in the event that there exists a serious and imminent threat to public health from the virus known as 'Wuhan novel coronavirus (2019-nCoV)'."

  - **Summary of legislation relating to coronavirus.** James Goddard, 'Coronavirus: emergency legislation' (House of Lords Library, 18/3/20) — This article describes the Health Protection (Coronavirus) Regulations 2020, the proposed Coronavirus Bill (which was introduced after the article's publication), and the Civil Contingencies Act 2004, and provides a list of further reading.

2.3 Parole Board

- **Legislation.** Parole Board Rules 2019 — The Gov.uk website lists the following as significant changes: (1) IPP licence termination; (2) New powers to release any prisoner on the papers; (3) Third party directions; (4) Appointing representatives; (5) Non-disclosure applications; (6) Decision on the papers after a case has been sent to oral hearing; (7) Decision summaries; (8) Reconsideration mechanism. Supersedes the Parole Board Rules 2016 (though those rules apply for parole reviews referred before 22/7/19).

3 Resources

All 2020 resources (including any added since this booklet was published) can be browsed on the database at: www.mhlo.uk/ci.

3.1 Mental Health Tribunal

3.1.1 Practice Directions

- **Tribunal coronavirus Practice Direction.** Pilot Practice Direction: Contingency Arrangements in the First-Tier Tribunal and the Upper Tribunal (Coronavirus, 19/3/20) — During the pilot period, initially six months: (1) decisions should usually be made without a hearing where the rules permit [MHT: rule 35 limits this to Part 5 and strike-out decisions, certain CTO referrals, and some urgent matters]; (2) in jurisdictions where a hearing is required unless the parties consent to a determination on the papers [MHT: certain CTO referral cases] Chamber Presidents may allow a paper "triage" scheme in which provisional decisions are provided in cases in which a successful outcome for the applicant/appellant is likely; (3) all hearings should be held remotely where it is reasonably practicable and in accordance with the overriding objective [MHT: rule 1 states that hearings may be "conducted in whole or in part by video link, telephone or other means of instantaneous two-way electronic communication"]; (4) where permitted, hearings will proceed in the absence of parties who have not made an adjournment/postponement application [MHT: a requirement of rule 39 is that the patient has decided not to attend or is unable to attend for reasons of ill health]; (5) tribunals will take into account the impact of the pandemic when considering applications for extension of time for compliance with directions or the postponement of hearings. [Notes in square brackets are not part of the PD itself.] Updated in June 2020 and superseded by Amended General Pilot Practice Direction: Contingency Arrangements in the First-tier Tribunal and the Upper Tribunal (Coronavirus, 14/9/20).

  - **Tribunal coronavirus Practice Direction.** Amended General Pilot Practice Direction: Contingency Arrangements in the First-tier Tribunal and the Upper Tribunal (Coronavirus, 14/9/20) — This extends Pilot Practice Direction: Contingency Arrangements in the First-Tier Tribunal and the Upper Tribunal (Coronavirus, 19/3/20), with some amendments, until 18/3/21.

- **Coronavirus tribunal composition (non-MH).** Pilot Practice Direction: Panel Composition in the First-Tier Tribunal and the Upper Tribunal (Coronavirus, 19/3/20) — This PD applies to all appeals and applications within the First-tier and Upper Tribunal, *except* in mental health cases. For the duration of the pilot period, initially six months: (1) a salaried tribunal judge may decide, having regard to urgency among other matters, may depart from the usual rules on panel composition; (2) in such cases, the tribunal may seek the advice of one or more non-legal members to assist with its decision-making, provided the advice is recorded and disclosed to the parties. Superseded by Amended Pilot Practice Direction: Panel Composition in the First-Tier Tribunal and the Upper Tribunal (Coronavirus, 14/9/20).

- **Coronavirus tribunal composition (non-MH).** Amended Pilot Practice Direction: Panel Composition in the First-Tier Tribunal and the Upper Tribunal (Coronavirus, 14/9/20) — This Practice Direction states that it applies to all appeals and applications within the First-tier and Upper Tribunal, except in mental health cases; however, the appointment of single judges under Amended Pilot Practice Direction: Health, Education and Social Care Chamber of the First-Tier Tribunal (Mental Health) (Coronavirus, 15/9/20) is said to be made under this PD. It extends Pilot Practice Direction: Panel Composition in the First-Tier Tribunal and the Upper Tribunal (Coronavirus, 19/3/20) until 18/3/21 with some amendments.

- **Mental Health Tribunal coronavirus Practice Direction.** Pilot Practice Direction: Health, Education and Social Care Chamber of the First-Tier Tribunal (Mental Health) (Coronavirus, 19/3/20) — For the pilot period, initially six months: (1) every decision, including those that dispose of proceedings, will be made by a judge alone, unless the CP, DCP or authorised salaried judge appoints two or three people; (2) the tribunal will suggest that CTO reference hearings are dealt with on the papers under rule 35; (3) it will not be "practicable" under rule 34 for any pre-hearing medical examinations to take place during the pandemic (no mention is made of video or telephone conferencing); (4) panels of one of two may seek the advice of one or more non-legal members to assist in decision-making, provided the advice is recoded and disclosed to the parties. Superseded by Amended Pilot Practice Direction: Health, Education and Social Care Chamber of the First-Tier Tribunal (Mental Health) (Coronavirus, 14/9/20).

- **Mental Health Tribunal coronavirus Practice Direction.** Amended Pilot Practice Direction: Health, Education and Social Care Chamber of the First-Tier Tribunal (Mental Health) (Coronavirus, 14/9/20) — This extends Pilot Practice Direction: Health, Education and Social Care Chamber of the First-Tier Tribunal (Mental Health) (Coronavirus, 19/3/20) until 18/3/21, with two amendments: (1) instead of "a judge alone shall make every decision unless the Chamber President [etc] considers it to be inappropriate in a particular case..." the new wording is "the provisions of the Composition Statement that apply to mental health cases shall be amended to include that a judge alone may make any decision (including decisions that dispose of proceedings) as directed by the Chamber President, Deputy Chamber President or an authorised

salaried Judge in accordance with Amended Pilot Practice Direction:
Panel Composition In The First-Tier Tribunal And The Upper Tribunal.";
(2) instead of "it will not be 'practicable' under rule 34 of the 2008 Rules
for any PHE examinations to take place" the new wording is "it shall be
deemed not practicable under rule 34 of the 2008 Rules for any pre-
hearing examinations to take place, unless the Chamber President [etc]
direct that in the exceptional circumstances of a particular case it shall be
practicable for such a pre hearing examination to take place, having
regard to the overriding objective and any health and safety concerns. ...".

- **Former STJs treated as current.** Pilot Practice Direction: The use of former
  Salaried Judges (26/3/20) — Former Salaried Tribunal Judges are to be
  interpreted as falling within the definition of salaried judges for the purposes
  of the coronavirus "Contingency Arrangements" Pilot PD.

- **Public/private hearings and access to recordings.** Pilot Practice Direction:
  Video/Audio Hearings in the First-Tier Tribunal and the Upper Tribunal
  (2/4/20) — (1) This PD, which applied to the FTT and UT, stated that
  (paraphrased): (a) where it is not practicable to broadcast a remote hearing in a
  court or tribunal building, the tribunal may direct that the hearing will take
  place in private; (b) where a media representative is able to access proceedings
  remotely then the hearing is a public hearing; (c) any such private hearing
  must be recorded if practicable, and the tribunal may consent to any person
  accessing that recording. (2) This PD had no impact on normal MHT hearings
  (which are private by default anyway). Also, following the Tribunal Procedure
  (Coronavirus) (Amendment) Rules 2020 amendments (which were inserted
  into the part of the rules which do not apply to mental health cases) there is no
  need to refer to this PD: see Senior President of Tribunals, 'Judges' and
  Members' Administrative Instruction No 4' (14/4/20).

3.1.2 Medical records

- **Automatic disclosure of medical records.** Mental Health Tribunal,
  'Direction for disclosure of medical records to legal representatives in all
  cases for the duration of the Pilot Practice Direction' (25/3/20) — Owing to
  the fact that representatives cannot arrange for patients to sign consent forms,
  this direction requires the responsible authority: (1) to allow immediate access
  to the patient's medical and nursing notes upon receipt of the CNL1 form
  containing the representative's name; (2) to email without delay any notes
  specified by the representative; and (3) to highlight any information in the
  notes not to be disclosed to the patient (the representative must not disclose
  this information without further order of the tribunal).

3.1.3   Community patients

- **Hearing postponement for certain community patients.** Mental Health Tribunal, 'Order and directions for all community patients who are subject to a CTO or conditional discharge and who have applied or been referred to the tribunal for the duration of the Pilot Practice Direction' (26/3/20) — (1) The hearings of certain community patients will be postponed, unless they have already been listed for paper review. (2) It applies to patients "over 18" (this is meant to mean 18 or over) presumably at the time of the application or reference. (3) The following will be postponed: (a) applications by CTO patients (s66(1)); (b) applications by conditionally-discharged (C/D) patients (s75(2)); (c) periodic mandatory references in the cases of CTO patients (s68(2) and s68(6)). (4) The following will not be postponed: (a) discretionary references for CTO patients (s67(1)); (b) discretionary references for C/D patients (s71(1)); (c) revocation references for CTO patients (s68(7)); (d) recall references for C/D patients (s75(1)). (5) The order purports to postpone periodic mandatory references for C/D patients (s71(2)) but these references are only made for a "restricted patient detained in a hospital". (6) The hearings will take place on the first convenient date after revocation of the Pilot Practice Direction, or earlier if the tribunal orders (the parties are to agree a new listing window after revocation and apply for a new date). (7) All parties are at liberty to apply to vary the order and directions in exceptional cases. (8) The reason given for the order is that (a) it is "not feasible or practicable for a community patient under the government's 'stay at home' policy to attempt to participate in a hearing"; (b) cases where the patient is deprived of his liberty are being prioritised for listing; (c) postponement is proportionate to the "extreme demands being placed on health, social care and justice services by the pandemic"; (d) the case will be relisted as soon as practicable "having regard to any temporary regulations or other priorities that may prevail during the coronavirus emergency".

- **MHT update including listing.** Mental Health Tribunal, 'Further update on coronavirus situation' (1/4/20) — (1) All hearings have been postponed for certain community patients (CTO and conditional discharge), unless they have already been listed for paper review, until the revocation of the coronavirus pilot PD, or earlier if the tribunal directs. (2) Section 2, conditional discharge recall, and CAMHS cases are the priority for listing; other cases were not being listed, but s3 and restricted cases should now begin to be listed. (3) Representatives are requested not to call the tribunal unless absolutely necessary, and to seek directions for late reports.

- **CTO hearings being listed again.** Conroys Solicitors, 'Listing of community hearings' (press release, 6/5/20) — It is understood that the order which postponed community hearings is no longer in force (the order stated that it was not feasible or practicable for a community patient to attempt to participate in a telephone or video hearing) and that the tribunal secretariat is working through the backlog.

- **Community hearings are now being listed.** Mental Health Tribunal, 'Order and directions for listing of community hearings' (6/5/20) — These cases had been postponed on 26/3/20 but now will be listed for hearing because the tribunal "has now achieved a level of administrative support to be able to list cases for community patients". The order and directions set out the duties on patients' representatives and responsible authorities in relation to reports, consideration of paper hearings, agreed hearing dates, and remote hearing practicalities.

3.1.4   Guidance for patients

- **MHT guidance for patients.** Mental Health Tribunal, 'Help for users' (15/4/20) — This guidance explains that hearings will be heard via telephone/video, by a tribunal judge alone ("because we have less support because of the coronavirus"), there will be no medical examination (because "people cannot meet together"), and community hearings will not take place ("because of the difficulties we have in organising hearings here everyone can participate" – unless the patient or representative explains "why your case must go ahead"). Superseded by Mental Health Tribunal, 'Help for Users' (updated, 28/7/20).

    - **MHT guidance for patients.** Mental Health Tribunal, 'Help for Users' (updated, 28/7/20) — This document was updated to reflect the situation as it was in July 2020. It mentions that "those cases that are listed for paper hearings under the usual procedures or cases where the patient has indicated through his or her solicitor that the detention is not contested ... are likely to be heard by a judge alone on the papers".

- **MHT guidance for young people.** RCPsych and Tribunals Judiciary, 'A Guide to Mental Health Tribunals for Young People' (11/2/16) — This document contains a simplified description of the tribunal process for civil sections.

- **MHT remote hearing CAMHS guidance.** Mental Health Tribunal, 'Important Information about your Mental Health Tribunal Hearing for CAMHS patients' (27/5/20) — This document explains remote hearings in simple language.

- **Tribunal guidance for patients.** HMCTS et al, 'Mental Health Tribunal: An Easy Read Guide' (22/7/20) — "This document will help explain what you can expect if you attend a face-to-face Mental Health Tribunal hearing."

- **Tribunal guidance for patients.** HMCTS et al, 'Mental Health Virtual Tribunal: An Easy Read Guide' (22/7/20) — "This document will help explain what you can expect if you attend a virtual Mental Health Tribunal hearing."

3.1.5 Guidance for psychiatrists

- **Guidance to psychiatrists about remote hearings.** Mental Health Tribunal, 'Message to the Royal College of Psychiatrists' (Sarah Johnston and Joan Rutherford, 26/3/20) — (1) This guidance to psychiatrists includes the following: all evidence will be taken before a tribunal judge alone, using phone (BT MeetMe) or video; the doctor giving evidence will released after giving evidence except in all but exceptional cases; the patient will not be given the decision orally. (2) To help the tribunal, clinical teams should: (a) submit s2 reports the day before the hearing (to avoid delays); (b) advise the tribunal judge if the patient will be unable to stay in the room or should give evidence first; (c) tell the tribunal judge whether the patient can remain as a voluntary patient (which is no longer possible in many areas); (d) emphasise any limitations of the evidence (for instance if the patient has recently been moved between "clean" and "dirty" coronavirus wards); (e) focus on the statutory criteria; (f) suggest delayed discharge for follow-up to be arranged; (g) give evidence from a private area. (3) The tribunal are encouraging wing members to return to clinical work, and are looking at formats for shorter reports.

3.1.6 Other guidance

- **MHT coronavirus guidance.** Mental Health Tribunal, 'Update on coronavirus situation' (18/3/20) — The position set out in this guidance is that: (1) hearings will continue as planned; (2) hearings require all three panel members, but this may change as part of the contingency plan being prepared; (3) requests to give evidence via telephone should be sent to the mhtcorrespondence email address; (4) hearings are being arranged as telephone conferences when hospitals are in lock-down; (5) listing window extension requests should be submitted to mhtcasemanagementrequests, but extended windows may be part of the contingency plan; (6) the tribunal is pushing for greater provision for paper hearings; (7) pre-hearing medical examinations are continuing, subject to the circumstances of each case, but these could cease if all hearings become telephone reviews. Largely superseded by: Tribunals Judiciary, 'Guidance from the Chamber President and Deputy Chamber President of HESC regarding the Mental Health jurisdiction' (Coronavirus, 19/3/20).

- **MHT coronavirus telecon procedure.** Tribunals Judiciary, 'Guidance from the Chamber President and Deputy Chamber President of HESC regarding the Mental Health jurisdiction' (Coronavirus, 19/3/20) — The following procedure will apply to hearings from Monday 23/3/20: (1) section 2 and conditional discharge recall hearings will be prioritised; (2) no pre-hearing examinations will take place; (3) new cases will be listed as a telephone conference before a single judge; (4) the judge can seek advice by telephone from that day's allocated medical or lay member, then repeat that advice in the telecon and allow submissions; (5) it is suggested that an unrepresented patient be allowed to speak to the judge without others in the room; (6) it is suggested that the decision is not announced.

- **MHT coronavirus update.** Mental Health Tribunal, 'Message from the Deputy Chamber President' (2/4/20) — This message includes the following information: (1) the tribunal is prioritising urgent hearings; (2) the administration should only be contacted if necessary; (3) the tribunal cannot currently make directions for reports.

- **MHT telephone hearing guidance.** Mental Health Tribunal, 'First-tier Tribunal (Mental Health) update' (2/4/20) — Information in this update includes: (1) all face to face hearings will be changed to telephone hearings for the foreseeable future; (2) the telephone attendee form, including the patient's number, is required 6 days before the hearing (24 hours for s2); (3) at the hearing the tribunal judge will telephone the patient with an invitation to join the call.

- **MHT video hearings.** Mental Health Tribunal, 'Video Conference Hearings' (6/4/20) — From 13/4/20 all cases will be listed as video hearings using the Cloud Video Platform (CVP), instead of telephone hearings. Telephone hearings had taken longer and made communication more difficult, and it is hoped that video hearings will be an improvement.

- **Further coronavirus guidance.** Senior President of Tribunals, 'Judges' and Members' Administrative Instruction No 4' (14/4/20) — This guidance refers to: (1) the Mental Health Tribunal, 'Help for users' (15/4/20) document; (2) the rule changes in Tribunal Procedure (Coronavirus) (Amendment) Rules 2020 (paper hearings, s2 timeframes, and public/private hearings); (3) plans for further or intermittent lockdown, the relaxation of lockdown restrictions, and both the return of existing business and new business; (4) paper case files; (5) some other matters irrelevant to mental health.

- **MHT remote hearings.** Mental Health Tribunal, 'Ensuring patients can access justice' (Sarah Johnston DCP, 22/5/20) — This article on the Judiciary website explains the adoption of remote hearing procedures by the MHT.

- **FAQs about HESC hearings.** Courts and Tribunals Judiciary, 'Frequently asked questions about hearing arrangements during the coronavirus pandemic – July 2020' (published August 2020) — There are FAQs about technology, hearings and mental health tribunals. (1) The technology questions are: (a) What is Kinly CVP? (b) How do I prepare for a Kinly CVP video hearing? (c) Can I test my connection beforehand? (d) I can't connect to Kinly CVP from my laptop/computer. What do I do? (e) What browser is best for Kinly CVP on my laptop or PC? (f) Can I use a smartphone? (2) The hearings questions are: (a) What if I want a friend to support me at the hearing? (b) What if my hearing requires interpreters or British Sign Language (BSL) interpreters? (3) The mental health questions are: (a) I would prefer to have a face to face hearing; can this be arranged? (b) I want to see the tribunal doctor before the hearing – can this be arranged? (c) I am a community patient and I cannot afford to join the hearing; (d) I need a full day's hearing; (e) I have had my case referred to the Tribunal but I don't want to contest it. What should I do? [Unrepresented patients referred to the tribunal "should contact the HMCTS ... and let them know that you are not contesting"!]; (f) Are the hearings private? (g) How will I be given the decision?

- **MHT video hearing guidance.** Mental Health Tribunal, 'Video Hearing Guidance for Participants in Mental Health Tribunals' (24/8/20) — This document contains the following headings: (1) To connect; (2) The hearing; (3) At the end of the hearing; (4) The written decision.

- **MHT video hearing guidance.** Mental Health Tribunal, 'Video Hearing Guidance for Representatives in Mental Health Tribunals' (11/9/20) — This document contains information under the following headings: (1) Before the hearing; (2) Listing hearings; (3) PHEs; (4) Uncontested References where patients do not want to attend a hearing; (5) Connecting to a video hearing; (6) The hearing; (7) At the end of the hearing; (8) The written decision.

3.2 Mental Health Review Tribunal for Wales

- **Welsh tribunal report PD.** Practice Direction: Statements and reports for MHRTs in Wales (October 2019) — This practice direction, which is based on and is similar to the English 2013 equivalent, sets out what is required of tribunal reports.

- **Welsh tribunal coronavirus PD.** Practice Direction: MHRT for Wales: Coronavirus COVID-19 (30/3/20) — This practice direction sets out the procedure for a period of 6 months. (1) During the pandemic, preliminary medical examinations will not be "practicable" owing to health risk. (2) Hearings will be held by telephone or video, unless dispensed with entirely (when a hearing would be impractical or involve undesirable delay, sufficient evidence is available to decide without a hearing, and this would not be detrimental to the health of the patient). (3) Tribunals will continue ordinarily to comprise three members, unless this is impractical or would involve undesirable delay, in which case a legal member may sit alone or with one other member.

3.3   Mental Health Tribunal for Scotland

- **Scottish MHT's coronavirus guidance.** Mental Health Tribunal for Scotland, 'Covid-19 Outbreak – Important Update' (19/3/20) — The MHTS intends to hold all hearings by teleconference from Monday 23/3/20. The update details how this will work in practice, including assisting patients to participate in proceedings.

3.4   Tribunal Procedure Committee

- **Tribunal rules consultation.** Tribunal Procedure Committee, 'Consultation on possible amendments to the Tribunal Procedure (First-Tier Tribunal) (Health, Education and Social Care Chamber) Rules 2008 on the timescale for listing Section 2 hearings' (from 11/2/20 to 7/4/20) — The TPC seeks answers to the following questions: (1) Do you agree that the requirement should be that the First-tier Tribunal lists all section 2 hearings within 10 days from receipt of the application notice rather than 7 days? (2) Do you have any other comments on this proposal?

- **Conclusion of s2 listing window consultation.** Tribunal Procedure Committee, 'Responses to the consultation (on changes to the s2 listing window) and reply from the TPC' (23/6/20) — The TPC made the proposed changes (10 days instead of 7 for listing s2 hearings), plus an explicit power to ignore the deadline. The change was a temporary response to the coronavirus pandemic, and its effects will be monitored before a a final decision is made. There were 60 responses, including from two organisations (the Law Society and the MHT Members Association): 51 were in favour and 9 against.

3.5   Court of Protection

- **Serious medical treatment guidance.** Practice Guidance (Court of Protection: Serious Medical Treatment) [2020] EWCOP 2 — "This practice guidance sets out the procedure to be followed where a decision relating to medical treatment arises and where thought requires to be given to bringing an application before the Court of Protection. The procedure is currently being reviewed within the revised MCA Code. That will, in due course, be subject to public consultation and Parliamentary scrutiny. This guidance is intended to operate until such time as it is superseded by the revised Code."

- **COP coronavirus guidance ("Guidance no 1").** Court of Protection, 'Visits to P by Judges and Legal Advisors' (The Hon Mr Justice Hayden, 13/3/20) — This guidance from the Vice President of the Court of Protection states that "visits should only be made to P where that is assessed as *absolutely necessary*", that "[a]lternative arrangements should always be considered first, such as telephone FaceTime and Skype conferencing", and that "[v]isits to care home are to be *strongly discouraged*" (emphasis in original). Judges should discuss any potential visits with the Regional Lead Judge, and keep informed of the advice on the judicial intranet which is reviewed daily.

- **Further COP coronavirus guidance ("Guidance No 2").** Court of Protection, 'Additional Guidance for Judges and Practitioners arising from Covid-19' (The Hon Mr Justice Hayden, 18/3/20) — (1) This guidance contains the following key messages (paraphrased): (a) hearings of less than 2 hours will be by telephone, but longer hearings will proceed unless the judge decides otherwise; (b) all practitioners must consider the range of options, including Skype and telephone conferences; (c) if directions hearings cannot be dealt with by agreement then a remote hearing should be sought; (d) every sensible effort to alleviate the pressure on court staff should be made; (e) further use of Skype beyond the current limited circumstances is being considered. (2) The guidance answers various questions in relation to: (a) acceptance of electronic signatures; (b) notification of P; (c) interim appointment of professional deputies; (d) service by email; (e) scanned documents and electronic bundles; (f) capacity assessments undertaken via video. (3) A "Core Working Group (COVID-19)" including judges and representatives of the (legal) profession will be set up to look at ongoing interim solutions.

- **COP guidance on remote hearings and serious cases ("Guidance no 3").** Court of Protection, 'Further Guidance for Judges and Practitioners in the Court of Protection arising from Covid-19' (Mr Justice Hayden, 24/3/20) — (1) The guidance on remote hearings is now: "as from today no hearings which require people to attend are to take place unless there is a *genuine urgency* and it is *not possible to conduct a remote hearing*." (emphasis in original) (2) Genuinely urgent and life/death cases will be identified and prioritised in the usual way, but if any difficulty arises the VP's clerk may be emailed.

- **HIVE group and 2m separation at court.** Court of Protection, 'Dear Colleagues letter' (Mr Justice Hayden, 23/3/20) — The "HIVE" group has been established, the objective being "to continue to refine our approach to dealing with the Court's business and to seek to ensure that it runs as smoothly as possible". It consists of: The Vice President; The Senior Judge, HHJ Hilder; Sarah Castle, the Official Solicitor; Vikram Sachdeva QC; Lorraine Cavanagh QC; Alex Ruck Keene; Kate Edwards; Mary Macgregor, Office of Public Guardian; Joan Goulbourn, Senior Policy Advisor, Ministry of Justice. All those who attend court should keep 2m separation from others at all times.

- **Detailed COP remote hearing protocol.** Court of Protection, 'Remote access to the Court of Protection guidance' (Mr Justice Hayden, 31/3/20) — This 20-page document confirms that no COP hearings which require people to attend are to take place unless there is a genuine urgency and it is not possible to conduct a remote hearing. It includes a template case management order, and sets out sets out operational protocols governing remote hearings under the following headings: (1) General; (2) Legislative framework; (3) Judicial access to audio/visual conferencing platforms; (4) video/visual Conferencing: (a) Cloud Video Platform MoJ/HMCTS; (b) Skype for Business; (c) Microsoft Teams; (d) Zoom; (e) FaceTime; (f) Lifesize; (5) Audio/Telephone; (6) Security; (7) Transparency; (8) Transcription/recording of the hearing; (9) GDPR; (10) Attendance of P at the remote hearing; (11) Litigants in Person; (12) Witness Evidence; (13) Electronic Bundles; (14) Use of Interpreters and Intermediaries; (15) Orders and Service; (16) Legal aid funding.

- **Remote hearing guidance for users.** HMCTS, 'How to join telephone and video hearings during coronavirus (COVID-19) outbreak' (8/4/20) — "Use this guide if you've been asked to join a hearing by telephone or video using BT MeetMe, Skype for Business or Cloud Video Platform (CVP) during the coronavirus outbreak."

- **Information about Hive group.** Court of Protection, 'Letter about Hive group' (Mr Justice Hayden, 4/5/20) — This letter sets out the aim and constitution of the Hive group, with particular focus on: (1) property and affairs; (2) welfare cases in the context of deprivation of liberty; (3) "community DOL" orders under COP DOL11; (4) transparency. The HIVE mailbox (hive@justice.gov.uk) can be used to raise coronavirus issues which do not relate to specific cases.

- **COP update.** Court of Protection, 'Court User Group Update' (HHJ Carolyn Hilder and Amrit Panesar, 21/5/20) — This letter to court users deals with the court's performance and activities during the coronavirus outbreak and some of the work being done to assist practitioners, under the headings: (1) Hearings; (2) Filing of form COP20s; (3) Electronic filing of P & A deputy applications; (4) Performance.

- **Care home visits.** Court of Protection, 'COVID-19 restrictions and the Court of Protection' (15/10/20) — "Of particular concern to us, in the Court of Protection, is the impact the present arrangements may have on elderly people living in Care Homes."

- **COPUG minutes.** Minutes of Court User Group Meeting (30/4/19) — (1) Apologies; (2) Minutes and Action points; (3) Court Manager's Report; (4) Update on the Mental Capacity Amendment Bills; (5) Response to correspondence; (6) Update on ALR scheme; (7) Contacting the court by telephone; (8) Update on progress of e-bundling; (9) COP9 papers not served; (10) COP General visitors using insecure IT equipment when visiting lay deputies; (11) Dealing with urgent applications; (12) Applications for authorities outside the standard terms of deputyship; (13) Request for consideration of a streamlined property and affairs process; (14) Amendment of property and affairs order templates to include reference to support for making decisions when P has capacity; (15) Naming solicitors in judgments;

(16) Any other business. Next meeting: 15/10/19 at 1400, at First Avenue House.

3.6 Her Majesty's Courts and Tribunal Service and Judiciary

- **Coronavirus jury trials guidance.** Lord Chief Justice, 'Coronavirus (COVID-19): Jury trials' (17/3/20) — (1) No new trial should start in the Crown Court unless it is expected to last for three days or fewer; (2) all cases estimated to last longer than three days listed to start before the end of April 2020 will be adjourned; (3) trials currently underway will generally proceed in the hope that they can be completed.

- **Proposed reduction on tribunal panel sizes (not MHT).** Senior President of Tribunals, 'Proposal to amend Composition Statements' (18/2/20) — This consultation relates to the General Regulatory Chamber, the Social Entitlement Chamber, the Property Chamber and the Health, Education and Social Care Chamber (SEND, Primary Health Lists and Care Standards cases only – not MHT). Consultation closes 14/4/20.

- **Telephone and video hearing coronavirus guidance.** HMCTS, 'HMCTS telephone and video hearings during coronavirus outbreak' (18/3/20) — This guidance on telephone and video technology has information under the following headings: (1) The decision to use telephone and video hearings; (2) Using existing technology and making new technology available; (3) The rules on using video and audio technology in courts; (4) Proposed legislation.

- **Coronavirus Family Court guidance.** President of the Family Divison, 'COVID 19: National Guidance for the Family Court' (19/3/20) — This guidance for all levels of the Family Court and in the High Court Family Division provides detailed guidance on remote hearings and states that "whilst the default position should be that, for the time being, all Family Court hearings should be undertaken remotely either via email, telephone, video or Skype, etc, where the requirements of fairness and justice require a court-based hearing, and it is safe to conduct one, then a court-based hearing should take place".

- **Coronavirus court guidance on remote hearings.** Lord Chief Justice, 'Coronavirus (COVID-19): Message from the Lord Chief Justice to judges in the Civil and Family Courts' (19/3/20) — This message states: "The rules in both the civil and family courts are flexible enough to enable telephone and video hearings of almost everything. Any legal impediments will be dealt with. HMCTS are working urgently on expanding the availability of technology but in the meantime we have phones, some video facilities and Skype." It contains some outline guidance in relation to social distancing, litigants in person, trials and hearings involving live evidence, prioritising work, possession proceedings, injunctions and committal hearings, civil appeals, and family matters.

- **Civil courts remote hearing protocol.** Judiciary of England and Wales, 'Civil justice in England and Wales: Protocol regarding remote hearings' (20/3/20) — "This Protocol seeks to provide basic guidance as to the conduct of remote hearings."

- **Tribunal coronavirus hygiene guidance.** Senior President of Tribunals, 'Guidance for tribunal judges and members – COVID-19 measures' (23/3/20) — This guidance covers matters such as 2m separation and hand washing.

- **Jury trials have been paused.** Lord Chief Justice, 'Review of court arrangements due to COVID-19, message from the Lord Chief Justice' (23/3/20) — (1) This message notes that jury trials cannot be conducted remotely and states that all jury trials will be paused for a short time to enable appropriate precautions to be put in place (this topic is only of peripheral interest to MHLO readers so please check the Judiciary website or elsewhere for further updates). (2) In relation to family and civil courts it confirms that hearings requiring the physical presence of parties and their representatives and others should only take place if a remote hearing is not possible and if suitable arrangements can be made to ensure safety.

3.7 Parole Board

- **Parole Board coronavirus guidance.** Martin Jones, 'Guidance to members' (Parole Board, 20/3/20) — The guidance from the PB CEO's Twitter account is: (1) The Parole Board is considering changes to guidance, so that fewer cases are directed to oral hearing. (2) The views of the prisoner or representative will be sought but the decision on whether an oral hearing is needed lies with the panel chairman. (3) At oral hearings, panel members, legal representatives, witnesses and victims may be allowed to undertake video/telephone links from home to try to avoid delay to hearings. (4) If one panel member cannot attend owing to coronavirus then the hearing should proceed wherever possible. (5) More cases will be concluded by a single panel member. See also: Parole Board, 'Further guidance to members' (1/4/20).

- **Parole Board guidance.** Parole Board, 'Further guidance to members' (1/4/20) — (1) A panel can now make these decisions at MCA (Member Case Assessment): (a) to release or recommend transfer to open conditions in appropriate cases on the papers; (b) to refuse release or decline transfer to open conditions in appropriate cases on the papers; (c) to direct a case to an oral hearing. (2) Members have the option to expand the panel if they wish. (3) The guidance includes factors to consider when deciding whether an oral hearing is needed.

- **Parole Board mental health guidance.** Parole Board, 'Guidance on Restricted Patients and the Mental Health Act' (v1.0, October 2020) — "This guidance provides information on the different types of transfers under the Mental Health Act 1983 (as amended 2007) and guidance to Parole Board members sitting in secure mental health settings. This replaces the following pieces of guidance: (1) Member Case Assessment Guidance – Annex 6 – Guidelines for MCA members on assessment of cases where the offender is held within a mental health unit (MHU) establishment. (2) References to the previous guidance have also been removed from: Oral Hearing guide – Chapter 1 – Pre-Hearing Issues (section 5)"

3.8   Care Quality Commission

- **Annual CQC report on MHA.** CQC, 'Monitoring the Mental Health Act in 2018/19' (6/2/20) — The Foreword to the report states that the CQC found: "(1) Services must apply human rights principles and frameworks. Their impact on people should be continuously reviewed to make sure people are protected and respected. (2) People must be supported to give their views and offer their expertise when decisions are being made about their care. (3) People who are in long-term segregation can experience more restrictions than necessary. They also may experience delays in receiving independent reviews. This is particularly true for people with a learning disability and autistic people. (4) People do not always get the care and treatment they need. Some services struggle to offer appropriate options, both in the community and in hospital. (5) It is difficult for patients, families, professionals and carers to navigate the complex laws around mental health and mental capacity."

- **CQC letter to providers about coronavirus.** CQC, 'Routine inspections suspended in response to coronavirus outbreak' (16/3/20) — The CQC has written to all registered health and social care providers stating that inspections will stop from 16/3/20 (except in a very small number of cases when there is concern about harm), asking to be notified within 24 hours of any suspected or known case or outbreak of COVID-19, and stating: "We encourage everyone to act in the best interests of the health of the people they serve, with the top priority the protection of life. *We encourage you to use your discretion and act in the best way you see fit.*" (emphasis in original)

- **CQC coronavirus procedure for SOADs.** Care Quality Commission, 'COVID-19: Interim Methodology for Second Opinions' (Dear Colleague letter, 20/3/20) — The summary stated in the letter is: "(1) We are asking mental health services to provide a summary of the patient's current issues to CQC when submitting a second opinion request, which SOADs will use instead of visiting the hospital to examine care records. (2) Consultations with professionals, including with the responsible clinician, will be undertaken by telephone or video (Skype or Microsoft teams). (3) Following telephone consultations, we will ask services to support patients who agree to speak with

SOADs to have access to telephones or technology to support a video call with the SOAD. (4) SOADs will not be asked to post original copies of certificates. We encourage services to accept electronic copies of certificates and act on that. The Government may lift the requirement for a paper copy, and we will issue further communications once this is confirmed."

- **Support for adult social care providers.** CQC, 'CQC sets out next steps to support adult social care during the COVID-19 pandemic' (15/4/20) — This document deals with (1) Personal Protective Equipment; (2) coronavirus testing procedures for staff; (3) statistics (from this week, death notifications collected from providers will include whether the person had suspected or confirmed COVID-19); (4) information gathering (data on coronavirus pressures from services providing care in people's own homes will now be collected).

- **Complaints procedure.** CQC, 'CQC has made changes to Mental Health Act complaints process' (11/5/20) — The CQC are prioritising MHA complaints from or about currently-detained patients; other complaints "will be reviewed, but may be paused during the coronavirus outbreak".

- **Annual CQC report on MHA.** CQC, 'Monitoring the Mental Health Act in 2019/20: The Mental Health Act in the COVID-19 pandemic' (26/11/20) — "This annual report on our monitoring of the Mental Health Act (MHA) puts a specific focus on the impact that the COVID-19 pandemic has had on patients detained under the MHA, and on the services that care for and treat them."

3.9 Ministry of Justice

- **HMCTS and MOJ coronavirus guidance.** HMCTS and MOJ, 'Coronavirus (COVID-19): courts and tribunals planning and preparation' (published 13/3/20 and updated periodically) — Advice and guidance for court and tribunal users during the coronavirus outbreak. This Gov.uk page is updated regularly, contains its own information, and also contains links to many of the relevant documents.

- **MHCS coronavirus update.** Mental Health Casework Section, 'MHCS Update: Covid-19' (Dear Colleague letter, 19/3/20) — This letter explains that MHCS staff are all working from home, their policies and procedures remain the same, and the ability to deliver casework is unchanged. If staffing levels decrease: the priorities will be recalls, prison transfers, upward transfers, tribunal statements and level/downward transfers and repatriations; there might be delays in leave decisions and discharges; and conditional discharge reports (CDRs) and applications for changes of discharge conditions (unless important because of risk) will be the lowest priority.

- **MOJ coronavirus update.** Ministry of Justice, 'COVID-19 Stakeholder Update' (22/3/20) — This email contains (among other things) clarification that the "key worker" category includes: advocates required to appear before a court or tribunal (remotely or in person); other legal practitioners required to support the administration of justice, including duty solicitors and lawyers and others who work on imminent or ongoing court or tribunal hearings; solicitors and barristers advising people living in institutions or deprived of their liberty.

- **MHCS coronavirus guidance.** Mental Health Casework Section, 'Q and A for healthcare professionals and MHCS staff' (30/3/20) — The questions are: (1) Will MHCS relax a requirement that supervisors should have face-to-face contact with patients living in the community, for conditional discharge reports? (2) What happens if a patient, who is detained in hospital, requires urgent treatment as a result of suspected COVID-19? (3) What happens if there is an urgent need to transfer a patient with suspected Covid-19 from one mental health hospital to another? (The document contains a new shorter transfer request template for use in this scenario.) (4) Is there still a requirement to submit Conditional Discharge Reports (CDRs) and Annual Statutory Reports (ASRs)? (5) How do I extend previously granted overnight leave at a community placement, to prevent the need for the patient to go back and forth between the hospital and community placement?

- **Coronavirus prison transfer guidance.** HMPPS and NHS, 'Prison transfers and remissions to and from mental health inpatient hospitals in relation to COVID-19' (28/4/20) — The headings are: (1) Context and principles; (2) Protocol for the pathway; (2.1) Referral; (2.2) Assessment; (2.3) Requires transfer and detention under the Mental Health Act 1983 (MHA); (2.4) Remissions from mental health hospital to prison; (3) Contacts for national escalation (if required); (4) Useful resources and links.

- **Sentencing proposals.** Ministry of Justice, 'A Smarter Approach to Sentencing' (CP 292, 16/9/20) — This document mentions mental health several times, in particular in relation to Community Sentence Treatment Requirements.

3.10 Department of Health and Social Care

3.10.1 Electronic forms

- **Statutory forms guidance.** DHSC, 'Electronic communication of statutory forms under the Mental Health Act' (27/11/20) — "An amendment to Mental Health (Hospital, Guardianship and Treatment) (England) Regulations 2008 allows many of the statutory forms under the Mental Health Act 1983 (MHA) to be communicated electronically. This guidance explains: (1) the circumstances in which statutory forms and other documents can be sent electronically; (2) best practice for sending them electronically; (3) general principles around sending, signing and storing electronic forms."

- **Electronic signatures.** Simon Lindsay, 'Digital mental health: Use of electronic forms and signatures' (Bevan Brittan, 31/3/20) — This article provides equivocal advice about the use of electronic signatures.

- **Electronic signatures.** Ross Tomison, 'Electronic Signatures and the Mental Health Act' (Thalamos, 20/11/19) — The conclusion of this article is: "The Mental Health Act doesn't require a signature to be handwritten. Provided all other formalities have been met under the act for the form which is being completed, then an electronic signature is legally valid."

3.10.2 Coronavirus

- **Department of Health coronavirus ethical guidance.** DHSC, 'Responding to COVID-19: the ethical framework for adult social care' (19/3/20) — The introduction states: "Recognising increasing pressures and expected demand, it might become necessary to make challenging decisions on how to redirect resources where they are most needed and to prioritise individual care needs. This framework intends to serve as a guide for these types of decisions and reinforce that consideration of any potential harm that might be suffered, and the needs of all individuals, are always central to decision-making." There are eight values and principles: (1) respect; (2) reasonableness; (3) minimising harm; (4) inclusiveness; (5) accountability; (6) flexibility; (7) proportionality; (8) community. Under the "respect" heading it states that "those making decisions should ... where a person may lack capacity (as defined in the Mental Capacity Act), ensure that a person's best interests and support needs are considered by those who are responsible or have relevant legal authority to decide on their behalf".

    - **Article about coronavirus guidance mentioning MCA.** Alex Ruck Keene, 'COVID-19 and MCA – first guidance out' (Mental Capacity Law and Policy, 19/3/20) — This article contains brief comments on the following: (1) DHSC, 'Responding to COVID-19: the ethical framework for adult social care' (19/3/20); (2) HM Government and NHS, 'COVID-19 Hospital Discharge Service Requirements' (19/3/20).

- **Care Act "easements".** DHSC, 'Care Act easements: guidance for local authorities' (1/4/20) — "This guidance sets out how Local Authorities can use the new Care Act easements, created under the Coronavirus Act 2020, to ensure the best possible care for people in our society during this exceptional period." The first sentences of the changes (which are each followed by "however"-type sentences) are: (1) Local Authorities will not have to carry out detailed assessments of people's care and support needs in compliance with pre-amendment Care Act requirements. (2) Local Authorities will not have to carry out financial assessments in compliance with pre-amendment Care Act requirements. (3) Local Authorities will not have to prepare or review care and support plans in line with the pre-amendment Care Act provisions. (4) The duties on Local Authorities to meet eligible care and support needs, or the support needs of a carer, are replaced with a power to meet needs.

- **Coronavirus care home visiting guidance.** DHSC, 'Update on policies for visiting arrangements in care homes' (22/7/20) — "Directors of public health and care providers should follow this guidance to ensure policies for visiting arrangements and decisions are based on a dynamic risk assessment and minimise risk wherever possible." Superseded by DHSC, 'Update on policies for visiting arrangements in care homes' (updated 31/7/20).

    - **Coronavirus care home visiting guidance.** DHSC, 'Update on policies for visiting arrangements in care homes' (updated 31/7/20) — "Directors of public health and care providers should follow this guidance to ensure policies for visiting arrangements and decisions are based on a dynamic risk assessment and minimise risk wherever possible." Superseded by DHSC, 'Update on policies for visiting arrangements in care homes' (updated 21/9/20).

    - **Coronavirus care home visiting guidance.** DHSC, 'Update on policies for visiting arrangements in care homes' (updated 21/9/20) — "Directors of public health and care providers should follow this guidance to ensure policies for visiting arrangements and decisions are based on a dynamic risk assessment and minimise risk wherever possible." The only difference between this and the 31/7/20 version of the page is the addition of the following text to the top of the page: "For the latest care home visiting guidance please see the *Adult social care: coronavirus (COVID-19) winter plan 2020 to 2021*. This guidance will be updated shortly."

- **ASC winter plan.** DHSC, 'Adult social care: our COVID-19 winter plan 2020 to 2021' (18/9/20) — "Here we set out the key elements of national support available for the social care sector for winter 2020 to 2021, as well as the main actions to take for local authorities, NHS organisations, and social care providers, including in the voluntary and community sector."

- **MCA/DOLS coronavirus guidance.** DHSC, 'The MCA and DOLS during the coronavirus pandemic: additional guidance' (2020, regularly updated) — This web page contains the following main headings: (1) [Best interests] decisions; (2) Life-saving treatment; (3) Depriving a person of their liberty; (4) Hospitals and care homes; (6) Other settings; (7) Supervisory bodies; (8) Emergency coronavirus health powers. It was updated on 24/12/20 with information under the subheading "Offering a vaccine to someone who lacks the relevant mental capacity".

3.11 National Health Service

- **Coronavirus hospital discharge service requirements.** HM Government and NHS, 'COVID-19 Hospital Discharge Service Requirements' (19/3/20) — The covering letter states: "We face an unprecedented challenge in the weeks and months ahead to provide health and social care services that meet the needs of people affected by coronavirus (COVID-19)." The document summary states: "This document sets out the Hospital Discharge Service Requirements for all NHS trusts, community interest companies and private care providers of acute, community beds and community health services and social care staff in England, who must adhere to this from Thursday 19th March 2020. It also sets out requirements around discharge for health and social care commissioners (including Clinical Commissioning Groups and local authorities). ... Implementing these Service Requirements is expected to free up to at least 15,000 beds by Friday 27th March, with discharge flows maintained after that." In Annex A (The Discharge to Assess Model) the MCA is mentioned: "Duties under the Mental Capacity Act 2005 still apply during this period. If a person is suspected to lack the relevant mental capacity to make the decisions about their ongoing care and treatment, a capacity assessment should be carried out before decision about their discharge is made. Where the person is assessed to lack the relevant mental capacity and a decision needs to be made then there must be a best interest decision made for their ongoing care in line with the usual processes. If the proposed arrangements amount to a deprivation of liberty, Deprivation of Liberty Safeguards in care homes arrangements and orders from the Court of Protection for community arrangements still apply but should not delay discharge."

- **Guidance on learning disability and autism.** NHS, 'Clinical guide for front line staff to support the management of patients with a learning disability, autism or both during the coronavirus pandemic – relevant to all clinical specialities' (ref 001559, v1, 24/3/20) — The Overview states: "People with a learning disability have higher rates of morbidity and mortality than the general population and die prematurely. At least 41% of them die from respiratory conditions. They have a higher prevalence of asthma and diabetes, and of being obese or underweight in people; all these factors make them more vulnerable to coronavirus. There is evidence that people with autism also have higher rates of health problems throughout childhood, adolescence, and adulthood, and that this may result in elevated risk of early mortality". The following key points are discussed: (1) Be aware of diagnostic overshadowing; (2) Pay attention to healthcare passports; (3) Listen to parents/carers; (4) Make reasonable adjustments; (5) Communication; (6) Understanding behavioural responses to illness/pain/discomfort; (7) Mental Capacity Act; (8) Ask for specialist support and advice if necessary; (9) Mental wellbeing and emotional distress.

- **NHS guidance on MH law during coronavirus pandemic.** NHS, 'Legal guidance for mental health, learning disability and autism, and specialised commissioning services supporting people of all ages during the coronavirus pandemic' (v2, 19/5/20) — "This guidance provides advice and support to commissioners (clinical commissioning groups [CCG] and specialised commissioning), providers (CCG commissioned and specialised commissioned), health care professionals, social workers, Approved Mental Health Professionals, local authorities, experts by experience, clinical experts, and independent chairs for Care and Education and Treatment Reviews, as well as regional NHS England and NHS Improvement colleagues, to help with the local planning already underway. The guidance will also be helpful for other individuals and partner organisations, involved in the pathways of care, for people with mental health needs, a learning disability and/or autism, including police, prisons and Immigration Removal Centres (IRCs)." The main headings are: (1) Introduction; (2) Key messages; (3) The Mental Health Act 1983 and the emergency Coronavirus Act; (4) Operational considerations for use of the MHA; (5) Guidance on using the Code of Practice during the COVID-19 pandemic period; (6) The Mental Capacity Act; (7) The Care Act; (8) Specific considerations regarding restraint, restrictive practice and the management of people who refuse to isolate; (9) Escorting patients detained under the MHA, including those on Restriction Orders (Sections 41 and 49 MHA) to and from acute general hospitals; (10) Specific considerations for specialised commissioned services; (11) Specific considerations for learning disability and autism services; (12) Specific considerations for people with dementia; (13) Specific considerations for mental health, learning disability and autism and the Criminal Justice System; (14) Application of digital technology to Mental Health Act assessments; (15) Annexes: (Annex A) Resources that have been developed to support practice in mental health; (Annex B) Mental Health Casework Section; (Annex C) COVID-19 – Escorting patients detained under the Mental Health Act (MHA) including those on Restriction Orders (Sections 41 and 49) to and from acute general hospitals; (Annex D) Guidance on using the Code of Practice during the pandemic period: (a) Section 136 assessment; (b) Approved Mental Health Professionals (AMHPs) and responsibilities of Local Authorities; (c) The role of hospital managers' panel; (d) Mental Health Tribunal Hearings; (e) Medical Reviews of Seclusion; (f) Section 17 leave and visitors; (g) Access to Independent Mental Health Advocates (IMHAs); (h) Second Opinion Appointed Doctors service; (i) Electronic forms and electronic delivery; (Annex E) Checklist to support decision in line with the minimum standards and safeguards on the application of technology to the MHA assessments. Superseded by: NHS, 'Legal guidance for services supporting people of all ages during the coronavirus pandemic: Mental health, learning disability and autism, specialised commissioning' (v3, 30/11/20).

- **NHS guidance on MH law during coronavirus pandemic.** NHS, 'Legal guidance for services supporting people of all ages during the coronavirus pandemic: Mental health, learning disability and autism, specialised commissioning' (v3, 30/11/20) — This document's table of contents highlights changes since the previous version to the following headings (though there are also changes elsewhere): (2) Key messages; (3) The MHA 1983 and the emergency Coronavirus Act; (8) Specific considerations regarding restraint, restrictive practice and the management of people who refuse to isolate; (Annex F) Annex F: Guidance on the testing and isolation of people of all ages in in mental health, learning disability, autism, dementia and specialist inpatient facilities during the coronavirus pandemic. Superseded by: NHS, 'Legal guidance for services supporting people of all ages during the coronavirus pandemic: Mental health, learning disability and autism, specialised commissioning' (v4, 25/1/21).

- **NHS commissioning.** NHS England, 'Who Pays? Determining which NHS commissioner is responsible for making payment to a provider' (25/8/20) — "This revised Who Pays? guidance sets out a framework, for the NHS in England, for establishing which NHS organisation has responsibility for commissioning an individual's care and which has responsibility for paying for that care. It is published for implementation by commissioners from 1 September 2020." There are four appendices: "Appendix 1 sets out the full dispute resolution process. Appendix 2 provides advice on defining 'usually resident'. Appendix 3 is a one-page guide to what has moved where from 2013 Who Pays? to the 2020 version. Appendix 4, published separately in Word, contains templates for submissions made to the national team under the dispute resolution process."

3.12 NHS Digital

- **DOLS statistics.** NHS Digital, 'Mental Capacity Act 2005, Deprivation of Liberty Safeguards England, 2018-19' (21/11/19) — "These official statistics provide findings from the Mental Capacity Act 2005, Deprivation of Liberty Safeguards (DoLS) data collection for the period 1 April 2018 to 31 March 2019."

3.13 Public Health England

- **E-cigarette policy guidance.** Public Health England, 'Using electronic cigarettes in NHS mental health organisations' (4/3/20) — This document contains recommendations which were designed to provide a single reference point for NHS service providers to standardise smoke-free policies on the use of e-cigarettes. This guidance states that e-cigarettes are not covered by smoke-free legislation, that they are less harmful than smoking, and that 1 in 3 cigarettes smoked in England is by a person with a mental health condition. The headings are: (1) Summary; (2) Purpose of this advice; (3) Introduction; (4) The difference between smoking and vaping; (5) Current position of leading health organisations on e-cigarettes; (6) The evidence on quitting with e-cigarettes; (7) Recommendations for organisational policies; (8) Recommendations for care; (9) Next steps; (10) Other useful resources; (11) Case study.

3.14 Legal Aid Agency

- **LAA coronavirus guidance.** Legal Aid Agency, 'Coronavirus (COVID-19): Legal Aid Agency contingency response' (18/3/20) — This LAA web page is the main source of Legal Aid guidance, and contains links to various sub-pages.

    - **LAA contract guidance.** Legal Aid Agency, 'Coronavirus (COVID-19): contract management and assurance' (14/4/20) — This web page, which is a sub-page of Legal Aid Agency, 'Coronavirus (COVID-19): Legal Aid Agency contingency response' (18/3/20), contains information about working with contract management, reducing administrative activity for providers, office and supervisory arrangements, and quality mark accreditation. Under the heading "Designated Accredited Representatives in Mental Health cases" it states: "We understand the current situation may mean you are unable to meet the requirements of the contract regarding designated accreditation representatives, including where an individual is not able to meet the 14-hour requirement. You should document the reasons why, but we will not take any action in this situation. It will remain a requirement all advocates before the tribunal except self-employed counsel must be members of the Law Society's Mental Health Accreditation Scheme."

    - **LAA coronavirus guidance.** Legal Aid Agency, 'Coronavirus (COVID-19): working with clients' (14/4/20) — This web page, which is a sub-page of Legal Aid Agency, 'Coronavirus (COVID-19): Legal Aid Agency contingency response' (18/3/20), includes information relating to making Legal Aid applications, assessing financial eligibility where a client cannot attend, using digital signatures, client finances and contributions, approach to emergency certificates, and operation of the statutory charge. (1) In relation to assessing eligibility it states: "Where a client is staying at home, it may still be possible to collect evidence by email or post. Reasonable efforts to collect evidence should still be made and recorded, before assessing without evidence if that is not possible." (2) In relation to signatures the advice, since 24/3/20, has included: "In situations where it is not possible to get a client signature, digitally or otherwise, please make a note on the file explaining why, countersigned by a supervisor, and also make a note on the application/form when submitted to avoid delays or issues with processing. Please seek a signature at the earliest possible opportunity. ... [S]upervisor signatures may also be provided digitally to enable effective remote supervision, as long as they are clearly related to the relevant file notes."

- **LAA remote working guidance.** Legal Aid Agency, 'Coronavirus (COVID-19): remote working' (14/4/20) — This web page, which is a sub-page of Legal Aid Agency, 'Coronavirus (COVID-19): Legal Aid Agency contingency response' (18/3/20), includes information on the MHT level 3 fee: "Most Mental Health Tribunal (MHT) hearings will now be heard remotely. We can confirm the MHT Level 3 Fee will be payable where representation is carried out at a remote hearing intended to dispose of a case and would have ordinarily taken place in person."

- **Civil escape case claims.** LAA, 'Contingency Measure for Civil Escape Cases – Electronic Submission' (24/3/20) — As a temporary measure, the LAA are requiring that these be submitted electronically. The guidance document contains full details.

- **Guidance about LAA contract terms.** LAPG, 'Guidance on what the Legal Aid Contract and LAA COVID-19 Guidance Allows' (25/3/20) — This detailed guidance contains information under the following headings: (1) Your office; (2) Progressing Current Cases; (3) Potential New Clients; (4) Providing "Remote" Advice and Digital Signatures; (5) Means Assessment for Remote Advice; (6) Supervision; (7) Supervisor Absence; (8) Key Workers; (9) Speak to the LAA.

- **Adjournment fee for remote hearing.** Legal Aid Agency, 'Civil news: fee rules change for mental health remote hearings' (16/7/20) — (1) The LAA has amended the Standard Civil Contract 2018 to specify that the adjourned hearing fee may be claimed for remote hearings where the representative has incurred travel, advocacy or (if 15 minutes elapse since the scheduled or actual start time) provided that reasonable steps were taken to prevent those costs being necessary. (2) The new rule will be applied retrospectively.

3.15 Office of the Public Guardian

- **OPG procedure.** OPG, 'NHS and social care staff: check if a COVID-19 patient has an attorney or deputy' (7/4/20) — The Office of the Public Guardian aim to respond to requests: (1) in relation to coronavirus patients, within 24 hours, Monday to Friday, with weekend requests being prioritised on Mondays; (2) for other patients, within the usual 5 working days. Updated version: OPG, 'NHS and social care staff: check if a COVID-19 patient has an attorney or deputy' (5/2/21).

- **EPA registration guidance.** OPG, 'How to register an EPA during the coronavirus outbreak' (27/4/20) — "If you need to register an EPA now, you can still do so while observing government guidance on social distancing, self-isolating and shielding."

3.16 Official Solicitor

- **Official Solicitor coronavirus guidance.** Official Solicitor, 'Coronavirus update – property and affairs team' (19/3/20) — The Official Solicitor and Public Trustee Office is operating but, because all staff are working remotely and do not have access to anything sent by post, it is requested that all documents are sent electronically. In order to avoid administrative delay, attachments should be sent as clearly-labelled separate files rather than single large files.

3.17 National Confidential Inquiry

- **Suicide and homicide report.** NCISH, 'Annual Report: England, NI, Scotland and Wales' (13/12/19) — "The 2019 annual report from the National Confidential Inquiry into Suicide and Safety in Mental Health (NCISH) provides findings relating to people who died by suicide in 2007-2017 across all UK countries. Additional findings are presented on the number of people convicted of homicide, and those under mental health care."

3.18 Mind

- **Mind's legal newsletter.** Mind, 'Legal Newsletter' (March 2020) — This newsletter contains news under the following headings: (1) Comprehensive mental health service for children still a long way off; (2) Making decisions for someone with fluctuating capacity; (3) National inquiry into the use of restraint in schools; (4) CQC monitoring the Mental Health Act in 2018/2019; (5) New guidance for the Court of Protection; (6) The meaning of "long-term" in the definition of disability; (7) Veganism – Equalities and Human Rights issues in mental health settings; (8) Deloitte highlight poor mental health which costs employers billions; (9) Can an incapacitous patient still choose their solicitor? (10) New study about Community Treatment Orders

- **Coronavirus advice for patients, carers and others.** Mind, 'Coronavirus and your rights' (April 2020) — This web page contains links to further Mind resources on: (1) Coronavirus and social care rights; (2) Coronavirus and sectioning; and (3) Coronavirus and your mental health.

3.19 Representative bodies

- **Bar Council coronavirus statement.** Bar Council, 'Chair of the Bar sets out concerns to MoJ, HMCTS, the Legal Aid Agency, the senior judiciary, the Bar Standards Board and the Inns of Court' (18/3/20) — The Bar Council is "calling for a suspension of all in-person hearings across all jurisdictions, save in very exceptional circumstances where a video link or phone hearing cannot accommodate the interests of justice" for an initial 30-day period.

- **Law Society coronavirus guidance.** Law Society, 'Coronavirus (COVID-19) advice and updates' (19/3/20) — This guidance contains information under the headings: (1) Advice for employers; (2) Advice for firm owners, managing partners or senior leaders; (3) Advice for members visiting police stations, prisons or courts; (4) Advice for international firms; (5) Advice for conveyancers; (6) Advice for litigators; (7) Advice for legal aid firms.

- **Bar Council coronavirus guidance.** Bar Council, 'Coronavirus advice and updates' (March 2020, updated periodically) — This web page contains information and links under the hearings: (1) Bar Council guidance; (2) Bar Council statements; (3) Bar Council, LPMA and IBC advice bulletins; (4) HMCTS updates; (5) Legal Aid Agency updates; (6) General government guidance.

- **Coronavirus guidance for psychiatrists.** Royal College of Psychiatrists, 'Legal matters – COVID-19 guidance for clinicians' (March 2020, updated periodically) — This contains information under the following headings: (1) Emergency legislation and the Mental Health Act – not yet in force; (2) Update on the operation of Mental Health Tribunals; (3) Changes to SOAD procedures.

- **AMHP coronavirus guidance.** BASW, 'Information and support for AMHPs, AMHP leads and Principal SWs on the role of AMHPs during the Covid-19 pandemic' (25/3/20) — The introduction to this 11-page document states: "This information has been prepared by BASW, with support from the Approved Mental Health Professional Leads Network and the Chief Social Workers office to provide up to date information on the AMHP role as the country responds to the Covid 19 pandemic." This is version 1. Check the BASW website for updates.

3.20 Welsh Government

- **Welsh guidance hospital managers' discharge power.** Welsh Government, 'Coronavirus: guidance for Local Health Boards and Independent Hospitals in Wales exercising Hospital Managers' discharge powers under the Mental Health Act 1983' (14/4/20) — "This guidance is provided to assist Local Health Boards (LHB's) and Independent Hospitals in Wales exercising

Hospital Managers' discharge powers under the Mental Health Act 1983 (the Act) during this exceptional period."

3.21 39 Essex Chambers Newsletter

The following are the newsletters added to MHLO during 2020, but all the newsletters are available on the 39 Essex Chambers Mental Capacity Law Newsletter page.

- **Mental capacity law newsletter.** 39 Essex Chambers, 'Mental Capacity Report' (issue 101, February 2020) — "Highlights this month include: (1) In the Health, Welfare and Deprivation of Liberty Report: a tribute to Mr E; fluctuating capacity; improperly resisting a deputy appointment; DoLS, BIAs and RPRs, and finding the right balance with constrained resources; (2) In the Property and Affairs Report: the OPG, investigations and costs; e-filing for professional deputies, and a guest article about the National Will Register; (3) In the Practice and Procedure Report: the Vice-President issues guidance on serious medical treatment; an important judgment on contingent declarations; the permission threshold; and disclosure to a non-party; (4) In the Wider Context Report: brain death and the courts; deprivation of liberty and young people; (5) In the Scotland Report: supplemental reports from the Independent Review of Learning Disability and Autism; the Scott review consults; and relevant cases and guidance."

- **Mental capacity law newsletter.** 39 Essex Chambers, 'Mental Capacity Report' (issue 102, March 2020) — "Highlights this month include: (1) In the Health, Welfare and Deprivation of Liberty Report: a cautionary tale about re-using material for DoLS assessment and capacity complexities in the context of medical treatment; (2) In the Property and Affairs Report: an important case on the limits of powers of professional deputies to act without recourse to the Court of Protection; (3) In the Practice and Procedure Report: medical treatment – delay, neglect and judicial despair, developments relating to vulnerable parties and witnesses, and Forced Marriage Protection Orders under the spotlight; (4) In the Wider Context Report: Mental Capacity Action Days, when not to presume upon a presumption, and a number of important reports from bodies such as the CQC; (5) In the Scotland Report: the DEC:IDES trial. We have also recently updated our capacity guide and our guide to the inherent jurisdiction."

- **Mental capacity law newsletter.** 39 Essex Chambers, 'Mental Capacity Report' (issue 103, April 2020) — "Highlights this month include: (1) In the Health, Welfare and Deprivation of Liberty Report: the DHSC emergency guidance on MCA and DoLS, the Court of Protection on contact and COVID-19, treatment escalation and best interests, and capacity under the microscope in three complex cases; (2) In the Property and Affairs Report: the Golden Rule in (in)action and the OPG's 'rapid response' search facility for NHS and social care staff to access the register of deputies / attorneys; (3) In the

Practice and Procedure Report: the Court of Protection adapting to COVID-19 and an important decision on the s.48 threshold; (4) In the Wider Context Report: COVID-19 and the MCA capacity resources, guidance on SEND, social care and the MHA 1983 post the Coronavirus Act 2020, dialysis at the intersection between the MHA and the MCA and an important report on the international protection of adults; (5) In the Scotland Report: the response of the legal community to AWI law and practice under COVID-19, and an update from the Mental Health Law Review."

- **Mental capacity law newsletter.** 39 Essex Chambers, 'Mental Capacity Report' (issue 104, May 2020) — "Highlights this month include: (1) In the Health, Welfare and Deprivation of Liberty Report: the Court of Protection, COVID-19 and the rule of law; best interests and dying at home; and capacity and silos (again); (2) In the Property and Affairs Report: further guidance from the OPG in relation to COVID-19 and an unusual case about intestacy, minority and the Court of Protection; (3) In the Practice and Procedure Report: the Court of Protection adapting to COVID-19; remote hearings more generally; and injunctions and persons and unknown; (4) In the Wider Context Report: National Mental Capacity Forum news, and when can mental incapacity count as a 'status?'; (5) In the Scotland Report: further updates relating to the evolution of law and practice in response to COVID-19. We also note that 9 May 2020 was the 20th anniversary of the Adults with Incapacity (Scotland) Act 2000 receiving Royal Assent."

- **Mental capacity law newsletter.** 39 Essex Chambers, 'Mental Capacity Report' (issue 105, June 2020) — "Highlights this month include: (1) In the Health, Welfare and Deprivation of Liberty Report: the Court of Appeal presses the reset button in relation to capacity and sexual relations, and three difficult medical treatment decisions; (2) In the Property and Affairs Report: the impact of grief on testamentary capacity; (3) In the Practice and Procedure Report: a remote hearings update, and a pragmatic solution to questions of litigation capacity arising during the course of a case; (4) In the Wider Context Report: DoLS and the obligations of the state under Article 2 ECHR, the Parole Board and impaired capacity, and recent relevant case-law from the European Court of Human Rights; (5) In the Scotland Report: the interim report of the Scott Review critiqued."

- **Mental capacity law newsletter.** 39 Essex Chambers, 'Mental Capacity Report' (issue 106, July 2020) — "Highlights this month include: (1) In the Health, Welfare and Deprivation of Liberty Report: LPS delayed to April 2022; alcohol dependence and other capacity conundrums; stem cell donation and altruism, and when to come to court in medical treatment cases; (2) In the Property and Affairs Report: updated OPG guidance on making LPAs under light-touch lockdown and a face-off between potential professional deputies; (3) In the Practice and Procedure Report: a basic guide to the CoP; litigation capacity and litigation friends and observations about intermediaries and lay advocates; (4) In the Wider Context Report: capacity and the Mental Health

Tribunal, a change of approach to s.117 aftercare and lessons learned from a close encounter with triage; (5) In the Scotland Report: the Scott Review summary of responses to its initial survey and a response from the Chair to the critique in our last issue."

- **Mental capacity law newsletter.** 39 Essex Chambers, 'Mental Capacity Report' (issue 107, September 2020) — "Highlights this month include: (1) In the Health, Welfare and Deprivation of Liberty Report: updated MCA/DoLS guidance, the anorexia Catch-22, and two important cases on deprivation of liberty; (2) In the Property and Affairs Report: remote witnessing of wills, professional deputy remuneration and the OPG annual report; (3) In the Practice and Procedure Report: CoP statistics, short notes on relevant procedural points and the UN principles on access to justice for persons with disabilities; (4) In the Wider Context Report: the NICE quality standard on decision-making and capacity, litigation friends in different contexts, and a guest piece giving a perspective on living with a tracheostomy and a ventilator; (5) In the Scotland Report: the human rights blind spot in thinking about discharge from hospital in the context of COVID-19.

- **Mental capacity law newsletter.** 39 Essex Chambers, 'Mental Capacity Report' (issue 108, October 2020) — "Highlights this month include: (1) In the Health, Welfare and Deprivation of Liberty Report: updated DHSC MCA/DoLS COVID-19 guidance, the CRPD in the Court of Protection and spotting the signs of abuse; (2) In the Property and Affairs Report: two important cases about deputies and fixed costs and how to get financial deputyship applications right; (3) In the Practice and Procedure Report: s.21A applications and interim declarations; the limits of the court's jurisdiction; contempt proceedings and when not to recognise a foreign order; (4) In the Wider Context Report: new GMC consent guidance, Sir James Munby returns to the inherent jurisdiction, new CQC publications and relevant ECHR developments; (5) In the Scotland Report: a new Chief Executive for the Mental Welfare Commission, MWC publications, and what COVID-19 has revealed about ageism and disability discrimination."

3.22 Miscellaneous resources

- **Crown Court trials and sentencing.** Martin Picton et al, 'The Crown Court Compendium' (Judicial College, December 2019) — "The main aim of this Compendium is to provide guidance on directing the jury in Crown Court trials and when sentencing, though it contains some practical suggestions in other areas, for example jury management, which it is hoped will be helpful." Both Part I (Jury and Trial Management and Summing Up) and Part II (Sentencing) have content relevant to mental health law.

- **Victims and tribunals.** Julian Hendy, 'Victims and the Mental Health Tribunal' (UK Administrative Justice Institute, 10/3/20) — In this article

Julian Hendy (founder of the Hundred Families charity) argues that the Mental Health Tribunal "could easily be more transparent and accountable to victims if only [it] had the will do to so". He argues for less secrecy and more transparency (making comparisons with the Court of Protection's transparency pilot and the Family Court's transparency review) and a greater role for victims in the tribunal's decision-making process (by analogy with the Parole Board's post-*Warboys* measures and its welcoming of victim personal statements).

- **Academic briefing note about assessment of mental capacity.** Sophie Stammers and Lisa Bortolotti, 'Mitigating the risk of assumptions and biases in assessments of mental capacity' (University of Birmingham, 23/3/20) — "Mental health and social care professionals routinely assess the capacity of people to make decisions about their lives, in accordance with the Mental Capacity Act 2005 (MCA). The briefing note outlines how the functional approach to testing capacity in the MCA underdetermines decisions, describing the risks for stereotypes and assumptions to affect outcomes. It advocates for the need for specific training for professionals using the MCA to enable them to recognise the role of value judgements in capacity decisions, to mitigate the effects of stereotyping and assumptions, and to improve decision making."

  - **Summary of capacity assessment briefing note.** Alex Ruck Keene, 'Going beyond the Mental Capacity Act in assessing capacity: recognising and overcoming biases and stereotypes' (The Mental Elf, 26/3/20) — This blog post summarises Sophie Stammers and Lisa Bortolotti, 'Mitigating the risk of assumptions and biases in assessments of mental capacity' (University of Birmingham, 23/3/20).

- **Impact of coronavirus on operation of MCA.** Alex Ruck Keene and Rosie Scott, 'The COVID-19 pandemic, the Coronavirus Bill and the Mental Capacity Act 2005' (39 Essex Chambers, 25/3/20) — This article contains information under the following headings: (1) The Coronavirus Bill; (2) Non-Statutory Guidance; (3) Guidance from the Court of Protection; (4) Advance care planning; (5) Commentary.

- **Critical lay view of remote COP hearing.** Celia Kitzinger, 'Remote justice: a family perspective' (Transparency Project, 29/3/20) — This article is written from the perspective of the daughter of the patient in the video hearing in *A Clinical Commissioning Group v AF* [2020] EWCOP 16.

- **Social distancing and mental capacity.** Sian Davies et al, 'Rapid response guidance note: COVID-19, social distancing and mental capacity' (39 Essex Chambers, 31/3/20) — "The Court of Protection team have been asked to advise on a number of occasions since 17 March 2020 as to the legal position where a person ("P") lives in the community and declines to practice social distancing in circumstances where P does not (or may not) have capacity to make decisions about social contact in the circumstances of COVID-19. Clearly the consequences of P going into the community, as she ordinarily would, are (a) that she is at risk of contracting COVID-19, (b) that she may infect others, if she has the virus, and (c) that she may be in breach of the new police powers which have come into effect." Superseded by Sian Davies et al, 'Rapid response guidance note: COVID-19, social distancing and mental capacity' (39 Essex Chambers, 6/10/20).

- **Social distancing and mental capacity.** Sian Davies et al, 'Rapid response guidance note: COVID-19, social distancing and mental capacity' (39 Essex Chambers, 6/10/20) — "This guidance note provides an overview of the framework within which decisions need to be taken in England relating to social distancing and self-isolation in the context of those with impaired decision-making capacity, including about considerations of deprivation of liberty."

- **Coronavirus testing and capacity.** Alex Ruck Keene et al, 'Rapid response guidance note: Testing for COVID-19 and mental capacity' (4/5/20) — "The Court of Protection team has been asked to advise on a number of occasions as to the legal position in relation to testing for COVID-19, especially as testing (a) starts to be more generally available; and (b) is increasingly been rolled out as mandatory in certain settings. What follows is a general discussion, as opposed to legal advice on the facts of individual cases, which the team can provide. It primarily relates to the position in England in relation to those aged 18 and above; specific advice should be sought in respect of Wales and those under 18."

- **DOLS case law summaries.** Aasya Mughal and Steven Richards, 'Deprivation of Liberty Safeguards Case Law Summary' (May 2020 edition, 21/5/20) — This two-page document summarises selected domestic and European caselaw on deprivation of liberty. There is a newer version: Aasya Mughal and Steven Richards, 'Deprivation of Liberty Safeguards – case law summary' (October 2020 edition, 22/10/20).

  - **DOLS case law summaries.** Aasya Mughal and Steven Richards, 'Deprivation of Liberty Safeguards – case law summary' (October 2020 edition, 22/10/20) — This four-page document summarises selected domestic and European caselaw on deprivation of liberty.

3.23 Books

These books are available from the Books website page.

- **Medical treatment book.** Ben Troke, *A Practical Guide to the Law of Medical Treatment Decisions* (Law Brief Publishing, 2020) — This book is aimed not only at lawyers, but also clinicians and anyone with an interest in how medical treatment decisions are made.

- **MHA book.** Richard Jones, *Mental Health Act Manual* (23rd edn, Sweet and Maxwell 2020) — This is the book everybody needs to have.

- **Medication book.** *British National Formulary* (Pharmaceutical Press, 79th edn 2020) — This edition was published on 20/3/20. The book is updated every March and September.

- **Classic mental health law book.** *Larry Gostin, Mental Health Services: Law and Practice* (Shaw & Sons, supplement issue no 18, June 2000) — The full text of this book is available on Mental Health Law Online (scanned and uploaded in August 2020).

4   Legal Action article

The following article was first published in the March 2021 issue of *Legal Action* magazine and is reproduced by kind permission. As well as the annual mental health case law article, there are regular articles relating to the Court of Protection (by Doughty Street Chambers barristers), and mental health law and policy generally (by Mind's legal team). Subscription details can be found on its website at www.lag.org.uk/subscriptions.

Mental health case law: update

Jonathan Wilson considers mental health case law from the past year relating to coronavirus responses, change in status during proceedings, capacity to make an application, deprivation of liberty during discharge, and other matters.

4.1   Pre-hearing medical examinations

Tribunal Procedure (First-tier Tribunal) (Health, Education and Social Care Chamber) Rules 2008 SI No 2699 (the TPR) r34 requires that a pre-hearing examination (PHE), to form an opinion of the patient's mental condition, take place 'so far as practicable' in certain circumstances. Those circumstances are: proceedings arising from Mental Health Act (MHA) 1983 s2, unless the patient refuses; other proceedings, if the patient requests it; and when the tribunal otherwise directs. The rule is still in force.

4.1.1   First practice direction: no PHEs

Pilot Practice Direction: Health, Education and Social Care Chamber of the First-Tier Tribunal (Mental Health) (19 March 2020) stated the following:

> *During the COVID-19 pandemic it will not be 'practicable' under rule 34 of the 2008 Rules for any PHE examinations to take place, due to the health risk such examinations present.*

No mention was made of video or telephone conferencing, which by then was making oral hearings practicable, and which seemed an obvious answer to the question of PHE practicability.

4.1.2   First-tier Tribunal decides that remote PHEs are practicable

- *Re C*
  [2020] MHLO 48 (FTT),
  21 August 2020

In this case, a salaried tribunal judge of the First-tier Tribunal (FtT) refused to allow a PHE, because the practice direction stated that it was not practicable. There was no mechanism stated in the practice direction for seeking a medical examination in individual cases; however, the patient in this case sought permission to appeal under TPR r46. A different salaried tribunal judge treated the application as a r6(5) challenge to directions and decided that:

(a) the practice direction is subordinate to the rules and to the overriding objective;

(b) in video-enabled hearings with a full panel, a PHE *is* practicable by that means; and

(c) hearings and PHEs should be conducted remotely as, even if the hospital would allow access, the tribunal will not put its members at risk of contracting or spreading coronavirus.

In this case, the salaried tribunal judge directed that a PHE would take place by video link on the morning of the hearing.

It should be noted that FtT decisions, while useful for representatives and, by extension, for patients, do not establish legal precedent.

4.1.3   Amended practice direction: exceptional circumstances

Shortly after that decision was published, the FtT published a new policy, *Video hearing guidance for representatives in Mental Health Tribunals* (11 September 2020), that PHEs would not take place except in exceptional circumstances. That policy is now implemented in Amended Pilot Practice Direction: Health, Education and Social Care Chamber of the First-Tier Tribunal (Mental Health) (14 September 2020), which states at paragraph 8:

> *For the duration of this Pilot Practice Direction it shall be deemed not practicable under rule 34 of the 2008 Rules for any pre-hearing examinations to take place, unless the Chamber President, Deputy Chamber President or an authorised salaried judge direct that in the exceptional circumstances of a particular case it shall be practicable for such a pre-hearing examination to take place, having regard to the overriding objective and any health and safety concerns. An 'authorised salaried judge' means either:*
>
> > *a.   a salaried, or former salaried, judge of the Health, Education and Social Care Chamber; or*
> >
> > *b.   a salaried, or former salaried, judge assigned to the Chamber*
>
> *who has been authorised by the Chamber President or Deputy Chamber President to exercise the functions in this paragraph.*

The amended practice direction gave no guidance on what would be considered 'exceptional circumstances' and no reason for the assertion that PHEs in other circumstances were 'not practicable'.

4.1.4   Upper Tribunal decides what 'exceptional' means

- *EB v Dorset Healthcare University NHS Foundation Trust and Lord Chancellor*
  [2020] UKUT 362 (AAC),
  16 December 2020

In this case, the patient persistently pursued a PHE. Four salaried tribunal judges of the FtT either refused a PHE or upheld an earlier refusal, but permission to appeal was eventually granted.

A three-member panel of the Upper Tribunal (UT) decided that the amended practice direction cannot override the terms of TPR r34, and has to be interpreted, if possible, consistently with the rule. The UT found that such an interpretation is possible: circumstances are 'exceptional' if a PHE is practicable (being an exception to the provision deeming that it is not practicable).

The UT stated that health and safety concerns, as mentioned in the amended practice direction, are relevant, and would be relevant to practicability even if there had been no pandemic. Rule 2's overriding objective is also relevant, although it does not allow the tribunal to refuse a PHE for any reason unrelated to practicability (in particular, the amended practice direction can make no change to the existence of the r34 duty, the cases to which it applies, or the purpose of the examination; and the patient's ability to participate in the hearing is not relevant).

In response to a resources argument, the UT stated that the availability of the requisite technology for PHEs is relevant to the overriding objective and '[w]here that exists, a PHE need not necessarily have (and may well not have) any material impact on the tribunal's resources' (para 19).

On the facts, the FtT had unlawfully misinterpreted the amended practice direction by considering reasons unrelated to practicability. The patient had since been discharged, but the UT would have set aside the FtT's decision had she still been detained.

Comment: Before the UT's decision, FtT salaried tribunal judges had been interpreting the words 'exceptional circumstances of the case' according to their plain meaning: no statistics are available, but anecdotal evidence is that PHEs became as rare as hen's teeth. The decision that circumstances are 'exceptional' when a PHE is practicable should mark a return to the status quo ante, as it is a recognition that the amended practice direction adds nothing to r34 and that PHEs should happen whenever they are practicable. The only difference is procedural: instead of the medical member deciding on practicability having attempted a PHE, the salaried tribunal judges control this decision and have to decide on the papers in advance. The practice so far has been to direct that PHEs take place via the Cloud Video Platform (as with the hearing), on the same day as the hearing, and for the hearing to be listed for a whole day, although none of this is necessary.

It appears that, following the UT decision, PHEs are routinely being granted when sought (though not by default in s2 cases as is required by r34) but that some representatives are out of the habit of providing advice on this topic. It should be noted that the Legal Aid Agency (LAA) document, *Improving your quality in mental health* (v5, December 2020, published 4 January 2021) adds a new 'major concern' noted by peer reviewers:

Where there is no evidence of an informed discussion with the client about whether to seek a r34 medical examination in non s2 cases (para 7).

4.2 Postponement of community treatment order hearings

- *Re B*
  [2020] MHLO 18 (FTT),
  28 April 2020

Early in the coronavirus pandemic, a decision was made in *Order and directions for all community patients who are subject to a CTO or conditional discharge and who have applied or been referred to the tribunal for the duration of the Pilot Practice Direction* (FtT (Health, Education and Social Care Chamber) Mental Health, 26 March 2020) to postpone all hearings for adult community patients whose case had not yet been listed for paper review and whose case was a result of the patient's application or a periodic mandatory reference. The reasons given in the directions stated that it was 'not feasible or practicable for a community patient under the government's "stay at home" policy to attempt to participate in a hearing' and mentioned that deprivation of liberty cases were being prioritised. The order stated that parties were at liberty to apply to vary the order and directions in exceptional cases.

In this case, the patient had made an application to the tribunal on 24 January 2020, the first day of her detention under MHA 1983 s2. The tribunal's decision of 5 February 2020 not to discharge her was set aside on 14 February 2020. Delays occurred owing to the lack of a hearing loop system, which led to a further delay for up-to-date reports. The hearing was finally listed for 29 April 2020 but on 22 April 2020 was postponed under the coronavirus order and directions set out above. By this time, the patient had been detained under s3, then discharged onto a community treatment order (CTO). She challenged the postponement under TPR r46. A salaried tribunal judge of the FtT, in a non-binding decision, concluded that the hearing should go ahead given the exceptional circumstances.

Comment: Shortly after the publication of that decision, it was decided, in *Order and directions for listing of community hearings* (FtT (Health, Education and Social Care

Chamber) Mental Health, 6 May 2020), to list all postponed hearings because the tribunal had by then 'achieved a level of administrative support to be able to list cases for community patients'. That order and directions set out the duties on patients' representatives and responsible authorities in relation to reports, consideration of paper hearings, agreed hearing dates, and remote hearing practicalities. The backlog was cleared over the summer of 2020.

4.3   Paper reviews for uncontested renewals

There is a new power in new TPR r5A allowing the tribunal to dispose of proceedings without a hearing if the tribunal considers that the following conditions are satisfied:

(a)   *the matter is urgent;*

(b)   *it is not reasonably practicable for there to be a hearing (including a hearing where the proceedings would be conducted wholly or partly as video proceedings or audio proceedings); and*

(c)   *it is in the interests of justice to do so.*

This power was inserted into the rules of all FtT chambers by Tribunal Procedure (Coronavirus) (Amendment) Rules 2020 SI No 416 on 10 April 2020 and will expire on the same day as Coronavirus Act 2020 s55(b).

The power is, at the time of writing, being used to enable a judge alone to decide 'uncontested' reference cases on the papers without a hearing (*Frequently asked questions about hearing arrangements during the coronavirus pandemic – July 2020,* Courts and Tribunals Judiciary, published August 2020). The tribunal's position is that all detention cases are urgent, that it is not reasonably practicable for there to be a hearing if the patient does not want to attend and does not want to contest detention, and that it is therefore in the interests of justice to hold a paper review.

Comment: Automatic references to the tribunal exist as a safeguard for those patients least likely to make an application for themselves. A patient can withdraw an application (with the consent of the tribunal) but cannot withdraw a reference. Allowing these patients to opt for a paper review is not far from circumventing, for the tribunal's administrative convenience, the patient's inability to withdraw a reference. Unlike other responses to the coronavirus pandemic, it is unlikely that there will be an appeal against this policy in the short term, but representatives should not agree to paper reviews and should consider challenging such decisions if in future they become aware of them.

4.4 Remote hearings set aside

4.4.1 Unlawful refusal to adjourn telephone hearing

- *GL v Elysium Healthcare Hospital and Secretary of State for Justice*
  [2020] UKUT 308 (AAC),
  9 November 2020

The patient in this case resided in a self-contained flat, adjacent to the ward, with another patient. On the day of the hearing, he and his flatmate were advised to self-isolate because another patient had tested positive for coronavirus. The patient's representative sought an adjournment because of concerns that the flatmate could overhear. The tribunal refused to adjourn, proceeded in his absence and did not discharge. The patient appealed.

The UT held that it was wrong for the FtT to have proceeded with the telephone hearing because:

(a) the tribunal had, without investigation, assumed that the patient's flatmate could not overhear;

(b) the tribunal had improperly dealt with the patient's anxiety: either it had concluded, without investigation, that the anxiety was without foundation (when he had in fact previously been assaulted because other patients discovered his history), or it had believed the same anxiety would arise at a future hearing (when in fact it arose from the specific circumstances that day); the tribunal should have considered whether his anxiety was genuine and, if so, the impact on his ability to participate; and

(c) the tribunal had wrongly approached the adjournment request as if the patient had been concerned with the mode of hearing (ie, telephone) rather than the fear of being overheard that day.

The case was remitted to be reheard by a differently constituted tribunal panel.

4.4.2 Unfair video tribunal hearing set aside

- *Re D*
  [2020] MHLO 51 (FTT),
  15 October 2020

In this case, the patient's microphone had been muted for much of the time after giving her evidence at the outset because she 'would not stop talking'. The tribunal decided not to discharge her from MHA 1983 s2, and she appealed on the basis that she had not heard all the evidence.

On review, a salaried tribunal judge of the FtT decided that it was not clear whether the patient had had a reasonable opportunity to hear all the evidence that was given at the hearing, and therefore it was not possible to be sure that the patient had had a fair hearing. The judge gave the following advice:

> *It would have been clearer if the tribunal judge had gone back to the patient at the end of each witness and checked that she had heard and understood the evidence given, and indeed the patient's representative could have checked with her client at the conclusion of the evidence ...*

The judge also decided that muting the patient's microphone did not amount to exclusion under TPR r38. The decision was set aside and directed to be listed before a differently constituted tribunal panel. As noted above, FtT decisions can be helpful but set no precedent.

Comment: Both *GL* and *Re D* show that problems arising from the difficulties in conducting remote hearings can amount to an error of law and provide the patient with the opportunity to be heard at a further hearing.

4.5   Change in status during tribunal proceedings

4.5.1   From s3 to guardianship

- *AD'A v Cornwall Partnership NHS Foundation Trust*
  [2020] UKUT 110 (AAC),
  30 March 2020

When the patient had been transferred from MHA 1983 s3 detention to s7 guardianship, the tribunal had been wrong to strike out her case for want of jurisdiction. The tribunal's jurisdiction arose from the s3 application, and none of the subsequent changes (including a new right to apply to the tribunal, different tribunal powers, and different parties) affected that jurisdiction.

4.5.2   From s3 to s37 hospital order

- *GM v Dorset Healthcare University NHS Foundation Trust and Secretary of State for Justice*
  [2020] UKUT 152 (AAC),
  4 May 2020

The FtT had been right to strike out proceedings arising from a s3 reference when the patient was subsequently made subject to a s37 hospital order. It would be contrary to statutory policy (which does not allow applications to the tribunal during the first six months of a hospital order) if the tribunal were to retain jurisdiction under an application or reference that was made before the date of the hospital order.

Comment: *AD'A* and *GM* add to previous case law which established that the tribunal retains jurisdiction following any changes between s2, s3 and CTO, and following transfer from s3 to s7 (guardianship), but loses jurisdiction following a change from s47/49 (restricted transfer direction from prison) to s47 (notional s37).

4.6 Capacity to make tribunal application

- *SM v Livewell Southwest CIC*
  [2020] UKUT 191 (AAC),
  12 June 2020

The patient in this case made an application to the tribunal with the support of an independent mental health advocate (IMHA) and was represented at the hearing by counsel. The tribunal medical member's PHE concluded that the patient 'did not and has never had during her admission the ability to understand what a mental health review tribunal means' and that 'she did not understand that a tribunal could discharge her' (see para 23). The patient's instructions to the barrister on the morning of the hearing were that 'she did not need to attend the tribunal, but just needed to leave' (see para 24); she later decided to attend the hearing and walked by herself from the ward to the tribunal waiting room.

The UT had previously decided in *VS v St Andrew's Healthcare* [2018] UKUT 250 (AAC); February 2019 *Legal Action* 19 that the capacity required by a patient to bring proceedings before the FtT in its mental health jurisdiction is as follows:

> *The patient must understand that they are being detained against their wishes and that the First-tier Tribunal is a body that will be able to decide whether they should be released (para 19).*

If the patient lacks that capacity at the relevant time then the FtT should strike out the proceedings under TPR r8, which states:

> *(1) With the exception of paragraph (3), this rule does not apply to mental health cases.*
>
> *[...]*
>
> *(3) The tribunal must strike out the whole or a part of the proceedings if the tribunal –*
>
> > *(a) does not have jurisdiction in relation to the proceedings or that part of them; and*
> >
> > *(b) does not exercise its power under rule 5(3)(k)(i) (transfer to another court or tribunal) in relation to the proceedings or that part of them.*
>
> *[...]*

> *(5) The tribunal may not strike out the whole or a part of the proceedings under paragraph (3) or (4)(b) or (c) without first giving the applicant an opportunity to make representations in relation to the proposed striking out.*

Having regard to the above, the FtT in SM's case decided that she had lacked capacity to make the application when she had made it, and therefore the proceedings were struck out. SM appealed. The appeal was heard by a three-member panel of the UT because it entailed a direct challenge to the correctness of *VS* and involved an important point of principle.

The majority of the UT confirmed that the test for capacity set out in *VS* was correct (the minority view was that the patient must merely understand that she is in a place that she wishes to be free to leave): the first part of the *VS* test might be rephrased as asking whether the patient realises that she is not free to leave the hospital, and the second part requires only an understanding that the tribunal can authorise her to leave the hospital. On the facts, the FtT had not erred in striking out SM's case.

The UT judgment contains detailed procedural guidance, including:

(a) The hospital should alert the patient and representative, before the day of the hearing, that there are concerns as to capacity to make the application. In SM's case greater efforts might have been made to secure the attendance of the IMHA at the tribunal had concerns been raised earlier.

(b) If a patient regains capacity then the tribunal should consider inviting the patient to make a fresh application and, having abridged any notice requirements, proceed to hear the case there and then.

(c) Anyone can request that the secretary of state make a reference: this includes not only the hospital managers and IMHA, but also the tribunal itself. In a case in which the patient lacked capacity to apply but wishes to leave the hospital, it would be sensible for the tribunal to consider adjourning for this purpose instead of immediately striking out the case.

Comment: The procedure for seeking a reference involves sending Form T111 to the Department of Health and Social Care (DHSC). Up-to-date contact details can be found on Mental Health Law Online: www.mhlo.uk/bp. The government proposes in the white paper, *Reforming the Mental Health Act* (DHSC, 13 January 2021; consultation closes 21 April 2021), to create a new statutory power for IMHAs to apply to the tribunal to challenge patients' detention on their behalf (see also page 29 of this issue).

4.7 Public hearing and capacity

- *AR v West London NHS Trust and Secretary of State for Justice* [2020] UKUT 273 (AAC), 10 September 2020

The FtT refused to hold a public hearing, mainly because it found that the patient lacked capacity to make the decision to apply for and have a public hearing. The patient appealed.

In the earlier case of *AH (Albert Haines) v West London MHT* [2010] UKUT 264 (AAC), the UT had stated that the normal practice that tribunal hearings are held in private is justified, and stated (at para 44) that the relevant factors in deciding whether to direct a hearing in public are:

- *Is it consistent with the subjective and informed wishes of the applicant (assuming he is competent to make an informed choice)?*

- *Will it have an adverse effect on his mental health in the short or long term, taking account of the views of those treating him and any other expert views?*

- *Are there any other special factors for or against a public hearing?*

- *Can practical arrangements be made for an open hearing without disproportionate burden on the authority?*

In relation to the factors above, the FtT interpreted the first factor as requiring an informed choice and concluded that '[w]ithout being able to make an informed choice [the patient] cannot have a public hearing' (see para 15 of the present decision).

The UT held that this decision involved errors of law:

(a) patients who lack capacity are entitled to have their best interests put to the tribunal in support of an application for a public hearing, and have their views taken into account; and

(b) the relevant 'matter' for the purposes of assessing capacity is not merely the public hearing application but conduct of the proceedings generally, although lack of capacity in relation to the former entails lack of capacity in relation to the latter.

The UT noted that the four factors set out above may have acquired a significance that is not justified and are merely factors relevant to the ultimate test of whether a public hearing is in the interests of justice. The matter was remitted to the FtT to decide on capacity and whether to appoint a legal representative, and whether to hold a public hearing.

Comment: Public hearings continue to be extremely rare. The only known hearings are *Re Albert Haines* [2011] MHLO 169 (FTT), *Re Ian Brady* [2013] MHLO 89 (FTT) and *Re Jared Britton* [2013] MHLO 146 (FTT).

4.8 Reviewing appointment of legal representative

- *SB v South London and Maudsley NHS Foundation Trust*
  [2020] UKUT 33 (AAC),
  30 January 2020

Following a six-month reference made under MHA 1983 s68, the tribunal appointed a legal representative under TPR r11(7)(b). Three weeks later, and a week before the hearing, the patient instructed a different solicitor, who wrote to the tribunal, enclosing forms of authority and transfer, stating that the patient had capacity to appoint him, and asking to be placed on record as acting on instructions.

The first representative objected to the transfer on the basis that the patient still lacked capacity to 'instruct solicitors'. A tribunal caseworker relied on that objection to refuse to place the new solicitor on record. By then the hearing was three working days away so the patient continued with the first representative, but afterwards challenged the refusal to allow him his choice of solicitor.

The UT decided that the initial appointment was unlawful because the form on which it was made (Form MH6b) was deficient: the rubric did not mention the 14-day time limit for challenging a delegated decision under r4. If it had, then the patient might well have acted in good time so that his attempt to have a new representative put on record would not have been made too late to be resolved before the hearing.

The refusal to rescind the initial appointment was also unlawful: there was no guarantee that the proper decision-making process was carried out; the tribunal had not given sufficient weight to the presumption of capacity in the face of new evidence of instruction; it seemingly ignored the principle that the test of capacity to appoint a representative is lower than the capacity to conduct proceedings; and it had abdicated its decision-making responsibility by allowing the prior appointment to trump any other consideration by basing its decision purely on the appointed solicitor's objection and assessment of capacity.

However, the decision of the tribunal panel in not discharging the patient was not flawed in any material respect, and neither of the unlawful decisions were set aside as the patient had since been discharged.

Comment: Another illustration of the need to keep capacity under review, though in relation to the tribunal panel hearing the case, is *PI v West London Mental Health NHS Trust* [2017] UKUT 66 (AAC); February 2018 *Legal Action* 27.

4.9 Direction for all-female panel

- *Re A*
  [2020] MHLO 14 (FTT),
  10 February 2020

In this case the patient's Form HQ1 sought: 'Female only panel due to complex trauma history – will not be able to participate in her hearing at all if males are present.' The tribunal nevertheless booked a male medical member, refused a subsequent request for a female doctor because 'the patient cannot select the members of the panel', and a salaried tribunal judge rejected a challenge to that decision. The medical member had by then been replaced with a female (for reasons that are not given in the decision) but the patient sought permission to appeal the salaried tribunal judge's decision under TPR r46 as the issue might arise again.

The FtT judge decided the case under r5 case management powers rather than r46, and derived guidance from a social entitlement case, *CB v Secretary of State for Work and Pensions* [2020] UKUT 15 (AAC); September 2020 *Legal Action* 29, which noted (*obiter*, at para 23) that the issue would likely arise in two categories of case, 'appeals involving sensitive and uniquely female medical conditions' and 'cases raising cultural issues about the giving of evidence', and that the common thread is that such questions must be judged by applying the overriding objective rather than by characterising such requests as parties attempting to 'choose their own tribunal' (para 24). The arguments in A's case were more clear-cut as she would not otherwise be able effectively to participate in the hearing or the PHE.

It was directed the case would be heard by an all-female panel.

Comment: Although, as noted above, of no precedential value, this is another useful FtT decision, particularly given the likelihood that most mental health lawyers and tribunal judges would otherwise have been unaware of the *CB* case from the Social Entitlement Chamber.

4.10 Deprivation of liberty during conditional discharge

4.10.1   Court of Protection's approach

- *Birmingham City Council v SR; Lancashire CC v JTA*
  [2019] EWCOP 28,
  17 July 2019

This case involved two patients, SR, who would be conditionally discharged if a Court of Protection (CoP) order authorising deprivation of liberty could soon be obtained, and JTA, who for almost three years had been living under a condition that he 'shall not be permitted to leave his accommodation unless accompanied and supervised at all times' (see para 14).

The applications for court authorisation of deprivation of liberty were made by the local authorities under the *Re X* streamlined procedure (*Re X* [2014] EWCOP 37) but were heard by a High Court judge at an oral hearing in light of the Supreme Court decision in *Secretary of State for Justice v MM* [2018] UKSC 60; February 2019 *Legal Action* 17. That decision was that the MHA 1983 does not permit either the FtT or the justice secretary to impose conditions amounting to detention or a deprivation of liberty upon a conditionally discharged restricted patient.

The judge referred to HM Prison and Probation Service's Mental Health Casework Section guidance, *Discharge conditions that amount to deprivation of liberty* (January 2019), which was published in light of *MM* and provides for two approaches. For patients who lack capacity to consent to deprivation of liberty and whose risk is to themselves, the solution is to allow conditional discharge with deprivation of liberty authorised under the Mental Capacity Act (MCA) 2005. For patients who lack capacity and whose risk is primarily to others, and also for all patients who have capacity, the solution, if further treatment and rehabilitation could be given in a community setting, is to consider long-term MHA 1983 s17 escorted leave.

On the facts, both patients were in the former category – they supported, but lacked capacity in relation to, the proposed care plans, which involved deprivation of liberty concurrently with a conditional discharge, and those plans were in their best interests. The court therefore authorised the deprivation of liberty. The judge, *obiter*, stated that the guidance document's two approaches involved a false dichotomy that did not withstand scrutiny, as it is strongly in a patient's own best interests to be kept 'out of mischief' and thereby be assisted in remaining out of psychiatric hospital.

4.10.2 Mental Health Tribunal's approach

- *MC v Cygnet Behavioural Health Ltd and Secretary of State for Justice* [2020] UKUT 230 (AAC), 16 July 2020

The clinical team in this case unanimously supported the patient's conditional discharge from hospital, but the only way that the necessary treatment could be delivered in the community would involve a deprivation of liberty. The FtT would have granted the conditional discharge but refused to do so as it felt constrained by the Supreme Court judgment in *MM*. The patient appealed.

The UT decided that although, following *MM*, the FtT has no power to impose conditions that would amount to a deprivation of liberty, it must discharge a patient if there are means by which the patient's case can be appropriately dealt with under other legislation, and it does have the power to coordinate its decision with the provision of an authorisation under the MCA 2005. This could either be by what the judge termed the 'different hats approach' (the same judge sitting simultaneously in the CoP and the FtT) or the 'ducks in a row approach' (adjournment or deferred conditional discharge pending authorisation under the MCA 2005). The equivalent outcome could be reached for capacitous patients by using MHA 1983 s17 leave, so there was no European Convention on Human Rights (ECHR) article 14 discrimination in favour of incapacitous restricted patients.

On the facts, the FtT had misunderstood the *MM* decision and had been wrong to refuse to defer conditional discharge for a standard authorisation to be put in place. The UT directed the conditional discharge of the patient on a future date subject to conditions of residence, supervision and compliance with all aspects of the care package, with permission (for the patient, her responsible clinician or the justice secretary) to apply to the FtT for variation in the event of a material change in circumstances.

Comment: Much of the jurisprudence around ECHR article 5 in the mental health and mental capacity context suggests that it is a square peg being used for a round hole, but *SR* and *MC* show that a pragmatic approach can still benefit patients.

The *obiter* statement in *SR* that it is in a patient's best interests to be kept 'out of mischief' (which, in SR's case, included potential violence against women) is interesting as it would effectively coalesce MHA 1983 detention, which is based on risk, with MCA 2005 detention, which is based on best interests.

The conditions set by the UT in *MC* are surprising:

(a) the condition of compliance with 'all aspects of the care package' seems to offend against the principle in *MM*, as the care package would amount to a deprivation of liberty;

(b) a conditional discharge can be deferred under MHA 1983 s73(7) 'until such arrangements as appear to the tribunal to be necessary for that purpose have been made to its satisfaction' but there is no power to defer conditional discharge to a specified future date, as the UT purported to do here; and

(c) the 'permission to apply' provision must only have been meant to apply before the future date, as after conditional discharge the patient cannot apply until 12 months have lapsed, the responsible clinician can never apply, and the justice secretary would not need to refer as he has his own power to vary conditions.

In the white paper, *Reforming the Mental Health Act* (see above), the government proposes a new power of 'supervised discharge', which would enable a restricted patient to be discharged with conditions amounting to a deprivation of that liberty (no similar change is proposed for CTO conditions).

4.11 Condition removed from conditional discharge

- *Re E*
  [2020] MHLO 52 (FTT),
  9 September 2020

The tribunal granted a conditional discharge but its written reasons contained an onerous condition – to abide by accommodation rules, sleep there every night, and not have overnight guests – that had not been discussed at the hearing. The patient appealed and, on review, a salaried judge of the FtT decided that there had been a clear error of law:

(a) the tribunal failed to provide reasons for imposing the conditions of discharge;

(b) it was required to provide a brief explanation;

(c) it was also required to announce the conditions that the patient was subject to in exact terms, which was crucial given that the patient was being conditionally discharged immediately.

The outcome was that the conditional discharge would remain in place but with the extra condition removed.

Comment: This decision is not binding, but the proposition that a patient being conditionally discharged immediately ought to be informed of the conditions upon discharge is common sense.

4.12 Other cases

4.12.1 Medical treatment

In *JK v A Local Health Board* [2019] EWHC 67 (Fam), 13 November 2019, the court decided that force-feeding the patient by way of nasogastric tube was treatment within the scope of MHA 1983 s63 because the refusal to eat was a manifestation or symptom of autistic spectrum disorder.

Similarly, in *A Healthcare and B NHS Trust v CC* [2020] EWHC 574 (Fam), 11 March 2020, the court decided that dialysis treatment, including the use of light physical restraint and chemical restraint if required, was s63 treatment as the patient's physical condition was a manifestation of his mental disorder.

4.12.2 Ex turpi causa

In *Henderson v Dorset Healthcare University NHS Foundation Trust* [2020] UKSC 43, 30 October 2020, the Supreme Court held that, although the trust admitted negligently failing to return the patient to hospital on the basis of her manifest psychotic state, which led to her stabbing her mother to death, the patient's claim for damages was barred by the doctrine of ex turpi causa non oritur actio (illegality).

4.12.3 Parole Board representation

In *R (EG) v Parole Board and Secretary of State for Justice* [2020] EWHC 1457 (Admin), 9 June 2020, the court decided that the power introduced in the Parole Board Rules 2019 SI No 1038 to appoint a representative 'where the prisoner lacks the capacity to appoint a representative and the panel chair or duty member believes that it is in the prisoner's best interests for the prisoner to be represented' (r10(6)(b), which is materially the same as TPR r11(7)(b)) could not be exercised in the absence of anything similar to the accreditation system operating in the MHT (combined with the LAA's pragmatic approach to the regulation preventing providers from making an application for legal aid).

4.12.4 Criminal appeals

Guidance on sentencing and mental health was provided in *R v PS, Dahir and CF* [2019] EWCA Crim 2286, 20 December 2019. The Court of Appeal substituted restricted hospital orders under MHA 1983 s37/41 instead of the existing life sentence in *R v Cleland* [2020] EWCA Crim 906, 16 July 2020, the imprisonment for public protection sentence in *R v Stredwick* [2020] EWCA Crim 650, 5 March 2020, and the MHA 1983 s45A hybrid orders in *R v Westwood* [2020] EWCA Crim 598, 6 May 2020, and *R v Nelson* [2020] EWCA Crim 1615, 2 December 2020.

Jonathan Wilson is a consultant solicitor at Campbell Law Solicitors and runs Mental Health Law Online (www.mentalhealthlaw.co.uk).

Printed in Great Britain
by Amazon

19145049R00052